WORK
here
NOW

MELISSA SWIFT

WORK
here
NOW

THINK LIKE A
HUMAN
AND BUILD A
POWERHOUSE
WORKPLACE

WILEY

Published by John Wiley & Sons, Inc., Hoboken, New Jersey.
Published simultaneously in Canada.

For general information on our other products and services or for technical support, please contact our Customer Care Department within the United States at (800) 762-2974, outside the United States at (317) 572-3993 or fax (317) 572-4002.

If you believe you've found a mistake in this book, please bring it to our attention by emailing our reader support team at wileysupport@wiley.com with the subject line "Possible Book Errata Submission."

Wiley also publishes its books in a variety of electronic formats. Some content that appears in print may not be available in electronic formats. For more information about Wiley products, visit our web site at www.wiley.com.

Library of Congress Cataloging-in-Publication Data is Available:

ISBN 9781119895275 (cloth)
ISBN 9781119895299 (ePub)
ISBN 9781119895282 (ePDF)

Cover Design: Wiley
Cover Images: Building: Wiley Arrow: © RLT_Images/Getty Images

SKY10038654_111722

To my husband, Artem, who changed my life, and my daughter, Mira, who changed my life again

And to my mom and dad, the clinician and the researcher, who taught me two equally valid ways of looking at the world

CONTENTS

LIST OF STRATEGIES

What to Do: Strategies at the Organization Level

Strategy 1: Regularly reexamine work for signs of being dangerous (directly or indirectly), dull and annoying, or frustrating and confusing.

Strategy 2: Don't take intensified work for granted—and don't be afraid to de-intensify.

Strategy 3: Question long-held assumptions and unintentional choices about work to revolutionize your DEI strategy.

Strategy 4: Seek to understand work, even if it's painful.

Strategy 5: Deliberately hold performative work in check.

Strategy 11: Unpack your foundational talent management assumptions—what decisions have you made on the basis of believing folks are lazy or slow?

Strategy 12: Regularly examine the jobs that impact your organization the most—have they changed in a way that affects how people's performance of those jobs looks (i.e., do they look lazy or slow because work is changing fast?)?

Strategy 13: Map how your customer experience and your employee experience interact.

Strategy 14: Tread carefully in how you talk about seamlessness and frictionlesness—internally and externally.

Strategy 15: Actively promote replacements for the anxiety monster and the boss baby customer.

What to Do: Strategies at the Team Level

LIST OF FIGURES

PREFACE

Bob: Looks like you've been missing quite a bit of
                     work lately.

Peter Gibbons: Well, I wouldn't say I've been *missing* it, Bob.

—*Office Space, 1999*

The world of work can seem to be an intractable beast. Whether you're running a team, running an organization, or running away from a soul-sapping job, all too often you may be slamming your head against your desk (literally or figuratively) as you ponder how to get work done well, humanely, and cost-effectively. It's a riddle wrapped within an enigma bundled up in complexity, right?

This book takes the opposite view. Fixing present-day work isn't easy, but it can be remarkably straightforward. If we're willing to look at the basics with a fundamentally human lens, we can begin to solve seemingly impossible problems like breaking historical productivity barriers or shaping a truly diverse workforce. Want to build a powerhouse workplace? Think like a human—at organization and team level. When brought to practical reality, statements like "Work shouldn't be boring" or "Job descriptions shouldn't rule out most of the workforce" can forever change how your organization or your team work.

This book focuses on two goals. The first goal is establishing language to speak about work problems you've likely long experienced but have never been able to fully articulate. Whether you're dealing with Boss Baby Customers or fighting the curse of performative work, being able to name the problem—and describe it to the stakeholders all around you—is often half the battle. The second goal is putting forth a toolkit of 90 strategies to address these gnarly workplace problems. You'll find these strategies at the end of every chapter. Forty-five of these strategies can be implemented at organization level—the macro view—while 45 take the micro view and can be implemented at team level. There's no "right" set of strategies, or right order to implement them in, only what's effective for your organization or your team as you test and learn in real time.

The insight from this book comes both from my own work across my career and the insights of my colleagues across Mercer, the more than 75-year-old consultancy redefining the world of work, reshaping retirement and investment outcomes, and unlocking real health and well-being. In Mercer's work with organizations, we find that embracing an array of strategies in a coordinated fashion generally trumps a single-point approach. People problems are more like a friendship bracelet, with many strands woven together, than a single-piece metal bangle.

How do we unravel the problems of the present and weave a new future? We'll start by learning the language of the ways work is broken, and then dive into how, having named the problem, we can begin to use a humanistic lens to fix it. We'll then meet a couple of nefarious characters—the Work Anxiety Monster and the Boss Baby Customer—whose efforts deform even the best workplaces. Having slain some monsters, we'll take a sledgehammer to the Workforce Copy Machine—the mechanisms that keep the future of work looking a lot like the past. From there, we'll look at a couple of basic resets that powerfully change how work gets done: making decisions in a more human way and thinking about populations instead of individuals. We'll then examine a trio of underappreciated forces (immigration, migration, and incarceration) that might be affecting your workforce and workplace far more than you thought. We'll also examine how to think about technology such that it works for, not against, your human workers—and we'll talk about how to stop humans from undermining themselves via greedy work, *Animal Farm* syndrome, and organizational structures and processes that ask too much of them. Finally, we'll turn our eyes toward the end of the rainbow: What does a real, attainable, future of work that works for both employers and employees look like?

It's going to be a fun, thought-provoking, and deeply practical journey. I'm thrilled you're along for the ride.

1 The Great Work Unpack

Understanding and Fixing Broken Work

"That for a man to be the whole of his life hopelessly engaged in performing one repulsive and never-ending task, is an arrangement fit enough for the hell imagined by theologians, but scarcely fit for any other form of society."

—William Morris, *Useful Work and Useless Toil,* 1885

Work sucks.

It's important that we start there, because part of what's gone wrong, across centuries and continents, is that we've shied away from this fundamental truth. We've gone after a monstrous problem with carefully chosen words and some light waving of hands, when what we actually needed to do was stake it through the heart, cut its head off, stuff the head with garlic, and expose the mangled corpse to the sunlight so it could catch fire and evaporate.

You might read this and say, "Work doesn't suck! I love my job." Many folks do love their jobs—but at any time, according to Mercer's data from our employee listening work with more than 8 million employees over decades, nearly a third of workers are *seriously* thinking about quitting. And those are just the folks who've been pushed to the point of no return.

For the rest of us, even when we're most excited about work, the dirty little secret is we kind of hate it too. I love my job—leading Transformation Solutions in North America for Mercer; I get to partner with brilliant, deeply kind colleagues to help an array of interesting organizations reshape their workforces and ways of working for the future.

But part of why I love my job is the opportunity to fix all of the things about work that I know are absolutely awful. Throughout my career, I've seen it all, across large and small firms, great and terrible leaders, and an ever-blossoming array of tech successes and failures. I've worked to solve hairy, gnarly workplace problems for my clients, but also, all too often, for my own teams. For every triumph, there are a million frustrations, and I've been plagued for decades with the sense that *we could do this all better*.

As we grapple with the seismic changes in work that have come with the COVID-19 pandemic, the silver lining to a dark cloud that has killed millions may be that we have a once-in-several-generations opportunity to genuinely reset how we work.

My personal epiphany about work came in the spring of 2020. COVID-19 had turned the city I love into a horror movie—empty and silent, with sirens wailing all night. My husband works in air cargo, so as shoppers moved from buying in person to buying online, demand for his company's services boomed, and he found himself working 24/7. My daughter's kindergarten was being taught virtually, which we now know is barely possible for that age group. At my former employer, we'd experienced layoffs, furloughs, and pay cuts. I was tapped to lead two series of global webinars, which I did from my dark bedroom, sitting in a teeny chair with my computer propped on a squeaking, uneven end table that threatened every day to tip over and cause an electronics disaster (see Figure 1.1).

Figure 1.1   My March 2020 desk setup

One day, sitting in the gloom with my computer swaying back and forth on the precarious end table, trying to juggle the chaos of creating just-in-time business commentary on a set of conditions frankly none of us knew how to manage even as I tried to shepherd a 5-year-old trying to properly draw an outline of her own face, a moment of pure terror came over me. What if I couldn't actually do this? Was this the moment when I tapped out? An anxious voice was loud in my head: "You're not good enough. If you were more organized, more dedicated, a better worker, a better mom. . ., this wouldn't be so tough."

Luckily for me, some survival instinct kicked in, and I stopped gaslighting myself. Was the problem me, or was it. . .oh. . . . I don't know. . .the global pandemic? For sure. But the problem was also a way of working—across every organization in the world—that operated like a battering ram, even when confronted with obstacles that were not necessarily in its power to knock down. "Let's all just pull together and push through" seems to work great until you can feel it not working. There's a seminal moment in *The Wizard of Oz* when the average man pretending to be a great wizard is revealed, and he screams, "Pay no attention to that man behind the curtain!" This was that moment for me—I saw the way we work for what it was, a collection of human foibles, absent of any true magic.

Once you start to see a way of working that doesn't work, you can't unsee it. Horror rose up for me in the most banal moments. One day a few months later I was on the phone with two beloved coworkers. I was cooking fried rice for lunch for the family, all still stuck at home, and they were sitting in front of their video cameras. I had a moment of total cognitive dissonance that spiraled and spiraled: Why are these guys on video? We all know what we look like! Why are we in this meeting? Should this have been an email? Why can't I find 15 minutes in my day to just fry some rice in peace? Are we doing this all wrong?

The ongoing labor crisis makes it clear: we are. With workers walking away from their jobs in droves, we no longer have the option to just keep muddling through. The Great Resignation has led to record-high quit rates in the United States—with more than 4 million Americans leaving their jobs each month in 2021, a historic high.[1] Frankly, we should have stopped muddling a long time ago. Even with the incredible technological gains of the last 40 years, the Bureau of Labor Statistics estimates that business productivity grows *less than 3% a decade*.[2] We've had winners and losers—companies have skyrocketed or gone out of business—but on a basic level, we're not getting things done any better than we did a generation ago. Companies are finally acknowledging people are hitting their breaking point too—a MercerMarsh Benefits survey from during the pandemic period showed that employers thought workforce exhaustion was a top-five people risk. Before the Great Resignation, worker exhaustion didn't even blip on companies' radar.

This book makes a simple argument: maybe if *the everyday experience of work* sucked a little less, we'd get more done. Our inclination as folks analyzing a business—and it's not a bad one—is that we need to focus on the "big rocks" that mostly fill the jar of work, and not the "sand" that just fills in the gaps between the rocks. In general this is a good way to look at business and at life.

But let's think about one of the core properties of sand for a moment—it's abrasive. It really wears things down. That's what's going on with the long-neglected everyday experience of work—it's wearing workers down every day. Unintentional, unexamined choices lead to serial minor irritations that grind all of the edges off everyone, hurting workers mentally and physically, and over time dramatically diminishing the productivity of the organizations that employ them.

Admirably, organizations have begun to focus more on the employee experience, honing in on how critical life cycle moments feel. Are performance conversations robotic? Do first days feel perfunctory? When you get promoted, does it feel special? Do compensation and benefits feel like the bare minimum, or do you feel cared for? Trying to understand and improve the employee experience is a meaningful step forward—a critical acknowledgment that the happiness of employer and employee might be far more interdependent than we've admitted in previous decades. And it's necessary, but not sufficient.

Work Sucks

Examining and improving the everyday experience of work is a step we've been afraid to take. While employee experience analysis takes into account a million different aspects of being employed by an organization, the experience of work grapples with one issue and one issue only—how does it feel, day to day, *to actually do your job?* If we can crack the code on this one, the pent-up productivity gains will begin to flow at pace.

The everyday experience of work is in fact going wrong in three key ways: it's dangerous, it's boring, and it's frustrating and confusing. If you have a really terrible job, it's all three at once!

So let's start with all the ways work sucks.

Work Is Dangerous

Let's start with the lowest hanging fruit: work can suck because it kills you. There are two ways work can kill you: directly and indirectly. The direct route is easy to document: the Bureau of Labor Statistics (BLS) notes that in a normal (non-pandemic) year, someone in the United States dies at work about every hour and a half.[3] Heartbreakingly, about 12% of those deaths are suicides or overdoses. Twenty percent of those deaths occur in a job with a lot of driving involved—unsurprising in a country when car accidents kill more people than strokes, Alzheimer's, or diabetes.[4,5] And perhaps most shockingly, 9% of those deaths are murders—a subset of the more than two million people in the United States who experience some form of violence at work each year.[6]

Even as I was writing this book, shocking deaths occurred in the workplace. In December 2021, a terrifying T5 tornado ripped through three states, throwing debris 30,000 feet into the air—as high as planes fly. The monster tornado killed dozens of people from a candle factory in Kentucky and a warehouse in Illinois, who were tragically at work around the clock as organizations powered frantically through the pre-Christmas rush.

Work doesn't even have to kill you directly to kill you. The United Nations' labor agency attributes 2.8 million deaths each year to a bundle of work-associated effects (stress, long hours, disease),[7] while the World Health Organization (WHO) believes that nearly three-quarters of a million people around the world die every year[8] *specifically due to working long hours.* In the United States, researchers tied 120,000 excess deaths to a bundle of issues at work (everything from a lack of health insurance to poor work–life balance to organizational injustice),[9] which would put work in the running with car accidents as a top-five cause of death overall!

These statistics are depressing. But they should be energizing too, because in many, many, many cases these are *things we can fix*. With proper attention to work efficiency and financial wellness (particularly for part-time workers), no one should have to work excessively long hours—a discussion we'll examine in a further chapter. We may struggle to limit suicides or overdoses at work, but if we could really solve the puzzle of iffy, unreliable work technology (an issue we'll dive deeply into in another chapter), we could automate our way out of the most dangerous pieces of dangerous jobs (BLS statistics show workplace deaths concentrated just where you'd expect, unfortunately—fishing, logging, roofing, etc.).

We can stop work from killing you. We've made major progress already. It may sound awful that someone dies at work every 90 minutes, meaning about 16 deaths a day, but in 1911, the AFL-CIO estimates 100 workers died on the job *every day*.[10] In the 2020s, we're ready for another step-change in progress—the next generation of what it means to be "safe at work."

Work Is Dull

Remember when technology was going to save us all? Sweep up all the repetitive work, smooth off all of the rough edges of tasks, and catapult us into the charming world of the Jetsons where everyone worked by pushing a button?

Well, a funny thing happened on the way to Spacely Sprockets. Despite an absurdly accelerated rate of technological progress over the last 30 years, work remains soul-crushing and dull for many people. A 2016 Udemy survey of office workers cited that 43% were bored, and about half of the bored workers were bored more than half the week.[11] That's a lot of boredom.

We've long had clues that a more technologically advanced working world could actually make work duller. I don't agree with a lot in *The Communist Manifesto*, but Marx and Engels did have an eerily apt observation in their 1848 work about more machines in the workplace leaving crummy, low-paid work for humans:[12] *"Owing to the extensive use of machinery, and to the division of labour, the work of the proletarians has lost all individual character, and, consequently, all charm for the workman. . .as the repulsiveness of the work increases, the wage decreases."*

There's a decent insight here: technology doesn't just take away lowest common denominator work. When deployed thoughtlessly, technology and industrialization often *drive the reorganization of work* in ways that are not necessarily appealing. Technology thrives on repetition; humans don't. The idea is that technology takes on all of the repetition, but the reality is that it often forces humans into repetitive environments where the tech itself feels at home—and people's brains don't have enough to work on. Consider any highly automated environment: a data center, a factory. Are the humans doing creative work or empathic work, or are they doing relatively repetitive work? In virtually every case, instead of doing "more human" work, humans are just working similarly to machines.

In Chapter 5 we'll dive deeper into the tortured relationship between work and technology, but for now let's move on to the next way work sucks.

Work Is Frustrating and Confusing

What's the difference between "dull" and "frustrating and confusing"? "Dull" is "I can do this work, but it's repetitive/requires too little brainpower." "Frustrating and confusing" is "I want to do this work, but dumb things are preventing me from getting it done." We've all been there: the 37-step processes, the computer crashes, the boss who gives you a different mission every day. Everything from TPS reports and PC Load Letter to congressional filibusters. Everyone's got an ever-increasing list of "this job would be great if not for. . . ."

The statistics on frustration make those on boredom look like small potatoes. One stunning study of 7,000 office workers in Europe estimated that a full 97% of those workers were frustrated at work.[13] (At that point, I'm starting to question the mentality of the 3% who *weren't* frustrated.) What's driving folks crazy? The same bogeyman emerges: tech. According to a group of researchers across U.S. universities, 42% to 43% of time spent utilizing workplace technology is completely wasted.[14] As a friend of mine joked, we spend enough time dealing with technology failures and frustrations in the professional services space that it would make sense to have a billing code for it!

Critically, work being frustrating and confusing hits you right where it hurts—your workers who care the most. The more motivated someone is to do a terrific job, the worse they feel about being frustrated and confused on the way to doing it. And as we'll examine in future chapters, frustrating and confusing work puts an inordinate burden on human workers—asking them to do more and more with diminishing returns.

Okay, Work Sucks—But Why?

Now that we've got a decent working taxonomy of how work sucks, let's dive into an even more interesting question: *Why* does work suck? What are the underlying mechanisms making work dangerous, boring and annoying, and/or frustrating and confusing?

The answer is, again, threefold:

• Work has intensified—workers are challenged to do more with less.

- Work is misunderstood and often misattributed—no one understands what really needs to be done, and thus the wrong people get credit.
- Work is performative—symbolic action has overtaken meaningful action.

These categories may sound a bit academic. So to better understand what's going on in each, we'll look at data and real company experiences.

Is it Just Me, or Did This Get a Lot Harder? Work Intensification

You may not know the term "work intensification," but you've likely experienced it. Brunner, Prem, and Korunka put the phenomenon in simple terms: "Due to increased economic pressure, fewer employees must do more work more frequently in less time."[15] If you're a fan of the TV show *The Wire,* you might recall the repeated mantra about "doing more with less" that was lobbed at cops, teachers, and journalists alike across multiple seasons of the show and myriad plotlines—that's work intensification. Just as the cops, teachers, and journalists on *The Wire* struggled with the concept, contemporary workers have increasingly chafed at intensified work. Researchers cite negative impacts of intensified work, including everything from stress to reduced job satisfaction to conflict with family. . .and even suicide.[16]

We'll come back to the impacts of intensified work, but let's start by understanding what it is. To think about what intensified work looks like, consider the crazy milkshake trend of the mid-2010s. If you enjoyed eating or reading about food during that period, you couldn't avoid elaborate milkshakes—bedazzled with candy, cookies, or even entire hamburgers (see Figure 1.2). In the age of Instagram, they looked amazing. . .and they generally tasted terrible. They were either too sugary, too overwhelming, or just gross. (I like burgers. I like milkshakes. I don't want a burger *in* my milkshake.)

As organizations have gone through tech-fueled transformations, they've been unable to resist the urge to construct "crazy milkshake" jobs. It's not enough to do a thing anymore—you have to also track, and conform to, an elaborate array of tech-generated and monitored metrics around that job, and perhaps perform other "joblets" too. The metrics you're trying to hit may change opaquely and without warning, and there's not really any regard for how difficult the job was *before* the organization started augmenting it—similar to the fact that milkshakes already had 1,000+ calories before we started dumping the candy drawer and half the kitchen into them. There's also usually very little thought about how the tasks someone is being asked to do work *together*—a peppermint milkshake with a bacon garnish, perhaps, where the flavors might not suit each other.

Figure 1.2 Overloaded milkshake
Source: DIGICEL.

Researchers have in fact been somewhat mystified by why work has become more intense in the last few decades—the change may be attributable to anything from Lean approaches to production to increased collaboration to the enhanced ability of management to monitor work.[17] Work intensification also clearly manifests differently in blue-collar versus white-collar work. In a blue-collar environment, workers might be expected to pack more items per hour, to pick more strawberries, or to complete more rideshare trips. In a white-collar environment, work intensification is usually inextricably linked to the over-collaboration described so beautifully by thinkers such as Rob Cross, concretely showing up in endless streams of meetings, and of course the deluge of emails derided by researchers like Cal Newport.

The interesting thing about work intensification is that unlike phenomena like the growth of working hours, it can be a bit of a silent killer. We lack language to capture work intensification, struggling with questions like, "Why am I in so many freaking meetings?" and it often sounds like whining when we complain about our jobs just being somehow. . .harder. . .than they used to be. On the other side, there's a torrent of rhetoric about how the world is just a faster, rougher place than it used to be. If you had to take a shot of tequila every time someone mentioned the VUCA (volatile, unpredictable, complex, ambiguous) environment, at many organizations you'd be drunk before lunch. Everything is just more difficult than it used to be; therefore, your job is more difficult than it used to be! Work intensity isn't the problem; world intensity is the problem. . .or so goes the really problematic cultural narrative.

What if we told the story a different way? What if we said, "There's more work to be done, but there are many, many more people in the world to do it than have ever lived on Planet Earth. And more of those people have education, experience, and access to basic health provisions than ever before. Despite its foibles, technology is more advanced than it has ever been. And on a fundamental level, we're working in a more humane way than we ever did—having spent more than a century eradicating inhumane working practices like slavery, child labor, and deeply dangerous work."

When we tell the story differently, work intensification makes no sense. Throughout this book, we'll explore how we might de-intensify work—and get more done, more happily, as a result.

Your Boss Just Doesn't Get It: Misunderstood Work

Have you ever done a job that no one quite understands? That's been most of my career. The work that truly energizes me is usually "emerging work," new to the organizations doing it. From working as an account planner in advertising (a job that doesn't actually involve accounts or planning) to selling carbon credits for a multinational bank (cue audio: "What's a carbon credit?") to consulting on transformation, I've never had one of those "Playmobile figurine" jobs. You know—your basic banker, lawyer, firefighter, nurse—something that can be represented by a kid's plastic figure. My jobs have always been a little. . .weird.

The dirty little secret is, most work is weird. Even jobs you think you understand, you probably don't. My favorite example is firefighters, for whom only 4% of calls are fire related![18] Four percent! Doctors may spend 15 minutes with a patient, and then, research suggests, slightly more than that amount of time—16 minutes— dealing with electronic medical records.[19] And these are straightforward professions; get into knowledge work, and it can become difficult to even categorize time spent on things like "answering emails." Ask a knowledge worker what their job truly *is*, and you'll often get a convoluted answer—back when we used to go to cocktail parties, this drove a lot of smiling, nodding, and changing the subject. Ballard Spahr's Chief Diversity, Equity, and Inclusion Officer Virginia Essandoh gives a great example from the legal profession:

> I think people are surprised to know a lot of the corporate lawyering happens sitting behind a desk and a screen, and it is not always standing up in a courtroom, even for litigators. It is a paper war back and forth. I think that that surprises people, the importance of writing, persuasive writing. It's not the glitz and glamor of fancy clothes, smoking guns, and clever catch-phrases. It is the sitting behind your desk, shoes all over the place, trying to figure out how to write something persuasively.

—Virginia Essandoh, Ballard and Spahr Chief Diversity Officer.

The problem with work being weird is that it's then misunderstood. Importantly, if we don't know what's in it, we pick the wrong people to do it, and we give the wrong people credit for doing it well. Tomas Chamorro-Premisic writes compellingly about this phenomenon on the leadership level, noting that our stereotypes of what good leadership looks like actually cause us to select blustering, incompetent leaders, but in fact, the problem goes much deeper than leadership into everyday choices around talent. Let's think about the firefighter example: if we defined the job of firefighting as literally just fighting fires, our selection and promotion criteria would be pretty straightforward. You'd have to be physically strong, extremely fearless, and good at communicating, under crisis conditions, mostly with other strong, fearless individuals (your firefighting peers). But that's only 4% of the job. Of the calls to fire departments, 64% are emergency medical services (EMS) and rescue calls[20]—where an entirely different skill set is needed. On EMS or rescue calls, firefighters are called upon to communicate with a wide array of the population, be intellectually nimble problem-solvers, and show a great deal of empathy. If that's your mandate, you pick different folks—and you promote different folks to fire chief as well.

Making the connection between the actual work and the actual person who'd do it well can sound abstract, but if you've ever experienced it going wrong, it's pretty darn painful. Because I do extra-weird work, I've probably had more than my share of brushes with misunderstood work and wrongly selected individuals to do it. A very senior executive once handed me a list of "the big egos [I was going to have to] wrangle" to build a set of services. The executive was right about the egos, but absolutely none of those individuals, an all-male, almost exclusively white group of men in their 50s, was at all useful to the initiative. The group that ended up collaborating on the work—more female, younger, and more ethnically diverse—had totally different skills. Was the executive trying to be an anti-inclusive jerk? Nope. He just misunderstood the work, thinking that it involved building from a certain set of beliefs about client issues toward services, when in fact what we needed was experts in the underlying services who could adapt them toward the client issues. Seeing the work with clear eyes allowed me to bring in the folks who could do it really well.

The consequences of misunderstood work can run deeper than just diversity and inclusion failures. I have vivid memories of early-2000s friends in trading roles boasting about their bosses not knowing what the heck they did all day. . .right up until the entire financial services system blew up in 2008.

Understanding work—and then hiring, deploying, and promoting the right people—is a seriously difficult task. But it's one we have to get right in order to get to a true future of work.

All The Work's a Stage: Performative Work

When we talk about work, we love athletic metaphors.[21] A potential hire with a broad array of capabilities is an "athlete"; an Agile style of work utilizes "sprints." And when we talk about "performance," the primary image we often evoke is one of athletic performance—charging forward, sweating, pushing ourselves relentlessly to do our very best.

But what if performance at work—as measured in the
increasingly controversial discipline of performance management—
has more to do with the other kind of performance, the artistic kind?
As a Bartleby column in the *Economist* noted, "Theatre has always
been an important part of the workplace."[22] As technology has in
many ways rendered work less transparent—an impact exacerbated by
increased virtual and global work, even pre-pandemic—the
temptation and the need to perform, to "show our work" in the
vernacular of elementary school, have escalated. If you were a
bricklayer a century ago, your boss could see how many walls you'd
built in a day—no amount of clever acting could obfuscate that. If
you're doing white-collar knowledge work today, your boss may not
see your outputs with any regularity, let alone understand
their impact.

Performative work springs up to fill that gap in visibility,
everything from sending lots of emails to looking attentive in
meetings to boasting about being busy on social media. It's all of the
"look at me working!" behaviors that don't accomplish anything—
needless reporting, currying favor with leaders, even creating processes
that demand further performative work from others. You may not see
my work, but I'll create a performance that enables you to "see" it.

Performative work might seem dumb but mostly harmless, but it
actually causes major problems in three areas: it obfuscates who's
actually doing the work and who's good at it; it disadvantages already
disadvantaged groups, including both traditionally underrepresented
groups as well as introverts; and it wastes time on an epic level—
including stretching work long past sensible working hours. Let's
unpack each facet:

- *It obfuscates who's actually doing the work and who's good at it*. This
  is going to sound screamingly obvious, but performative
  work. . .is not work. By definition, anything we're doing to create
  a performance of work takes time away from actual work—and if

managers judge their teams by who's *performing* work well, they're often snubbing the folks who are actually getting anything done. This is perhaps why we have so many "unsung heroes" in workplaces—we've over-rotated on doing and rewarding performative activities, perpetually stranding the folks who are capable at the underlying work.

- *It disadvantages already disadvantaged groups.* It's bad enough that performative work disadvantages people good at the actual work. But even worse, highly performative workplaces will always ignore introverts (for whom this sort of performance comes less naturally) as well as other historically underrepresented groups. These groups may find that when work is judged on performative criteria, their performances are subject to terribly subjective judgments. I'm still reeling, many years later, from a colleague's comment that I did not want "to be seen as Little Miss Bossy." "To be seen" is doing a lot of work in that phrase—the critique wasn't about my work, it was about how I was being perceived (with a children's book character as the frame of reference, to boot!). For underrepresented groups, performative workplaces are exhausting minefields—you're dodging through shadows, with no anchor in real tasks or outcomes. It's all playacting and perception. Even if you can get into the playacting, engaging in performative work can create another layer of exhaustion for people already having to "perform" the behavior of white, male norms.

- *It wastes time on an epic level and elongates working hours.* Coming back to the notion that performative work is not work, from a productivity perspective you've got to wonder why we're doing it at all! Within large, complex, matrixed organizations, this dynamic can get particularly pronounced, as hordes of leaders scramble to prove their value to each other with elaborate, useless documentation and reporting of activity. . .and then hours of meetings to read those documents to each other. Even blue-collar workplaces have a version of this—when leaders seek "enthusiastic" employees, hours and hours of actual work time are wasted by, dare I say it, programmatic sucking up. The performance of work also routinely stretches working hours, as employees feel the need to be visibly "in the office" (physically or palpably online) to show how hard they're working.

What to Do: Five Strategies for Organizations

Throughout this chapter, we've looked at the different ways modern-day work glitches out—to the detriment of organizations and their workers alike. So let's get to "the good part"—what can you do, at organizational level, to start to create a more human way of working? Here are five strategies organizations would do well to employ—one, several, or all put together may truly unlock a better path to productivity and worker happiness alike.

- **Strategy 1: Regularly reexamine work for signs of being dangerous (directly or indirectly), dull and annoying, or frustrating and confusing.** Organizations that do openly dangerous work—coal mining, deep sea fishing, etc.—have strong monitoring and controls over this work, for regulatory reasons or through simple necessity. Most organizations, though, don't consider themselves to do dangerous work—and thus don't regularly examine the health impacts of their work. They're missing a trick on the employee retention front—Mercer research shows that employees who believe they are receiving good wellness support at work are far less likely to leave their job as a result.[23] And very few organizations actually routinely try to ferret out dull or frustrating/confusing work— taking the attitude "that's what we pay you for!" Bored, frustrated, or confused workers are definitionally unproductive workers—and organizations can't afford anymore to ignore this critical intersection between worker happiness and concrete financial goals.

- **Strategy 2: Don't take intensified work for granted—and don't be afraid to de-intensify.** Throw out false narratives about a VUCA world demanding 24/7 engagement—and examine work intensity in key roles with a jaundiced eye, paying special attention to where work intensity has crept in unintentionally. In concrete transformations—like an acquisition or the introduction of new technology—you may be able to spot an increase in work intensity. But in many other cases, work has just gotten harder over the years with no triggering event, which means in many cases it can be restructured to take far less of a toll on the employees who perform it.

- **Strategy 3: Question long-held assumptions and unintentional choices about work to revolutionize your diversity, equity, and inclusion (DEI) strategy.** Organizations deploy an array of strategies today—from more conscious pipeline management to a host of trainings—to try to establish a more diverse workforce and a more inclusive workplace. Major strides have been made, but a good deal of room for progress exists. Organizations can make up some of that ground by looking at problematic work—intensified, misunderstood, or performative—and fixing the underlying work problems. Intensified or performative work may stretch long into the night, disadvantaging caregivers (the Greedy Work issue we'll discuss in Chapter 8). If work is misunderstood, hiring and promotions may be less inclusive than they could be. Performative workplaces, as discussed, provide a strong advantage to already advantaged groups, as meritocratic concerns are elided or erased. Changing work is in fact the best DEI lever that's rarely tried.

- **Strategy 4: Seek to understand work, even if it's painful.** Working with clients on changes in work, you often hear, "Oh, God, if we start to unpack how that work gets done, it's going to be excruciating." Additionally, executives often fear deconstructing work where technology is heavily involved, for fear of their own lack of tech savvy being exposed. Despite these fears, the quest to understand how a particular job gets done is inevitably a productive one—often showcasing the fact that *no one* involved in a particular task of initiative understands the actual work.

- **Strategy 5: Deliberately hold performative work in check.** Work that is being done for show is the enemy of real productivity, in addition to the many associated DEI concerns. Organizations need to understand their worst performative work issues (working long hours for no reason, meaningless meetings, cultures of over-reporting, etc.) and tackle them head-on—actually calling out what's performative and what's real. The change starts at C-suite level, and boards can act as a useful check on whether performative work is really being addressed, or just being addressed. . .performatively.

What to Do: Five Strategies for Teams

Organization-level strategies are terrific and necessary—but the work of organizations, as we all see every day, gets done within teams. So throughout this book, I'll also provide strategies that can be used *within a working team*—creating progress at micro, not just macro level. Here are five strategies you can implement within your team, today, to change the way the team works:

- **Strategy 6: At a regular cadence, talk to your team about their everyday experience of work—what are they doing, and how are they feeling, day to day and minute to minute?** These conversations shouldn't be about the big picture—they should be about the details of their everyday work that might feel insignificant. Are there particular tasks that are seeming difficult? How much time are they spending in meetings? Is a particular technology helping them or slowing them down? Create a safe, nonjudgmental space where they can raise concerns that might feel trivial—and don't be afraid to probe on the little details.

- **Strategy 7: Quiet your "suck it up" voice.** We've all been there: someone on your team brings a concern to you and your brain starts screaming, "STOP WHINING!" Before you know it, you're down a deep rabbit hole of all the times in your career you tolerated the same thing or much, much worse. You tell the person to suck it up and deal with whatever's going on—the work equivalent of telling your kids you walked 6 miles to school in the snow. If you want work to change for the better, make that voice shut up, and consider the change you can make.

- **Strategy 8: Be humble and curious about the parts of your team's work you don't understand.** Long gone are the days when any leader would necessarily understand every aspect of their team's work. Career paths vary, and work changes fast; there is no shame in not fully "getting" the team's work. Leaders who can identify what of their team's work eludes their understanding— and who can ask about it without either feeling threatened or conveying threat to the team—can both help their team work better and avoid the risks posed by not completely understanding what the people who work for them do.

- **Strategy 9: Develop metrics to measure and monitor work intensity.** While it's important to reduce work intensity on an organizational level, team level is where the rubber truly hits the road. Figure out what metrics measure your team's work intensity—which could be anything from number of meetings in a day to number of production line emergencies to number of angry customers during a shift—and keep an eye on them. You may or may not always be able to de-intensify work, but at least you can provide supportive solutions at times when work becomes more intense. For instance, many professional services organizations (ourselves included!) have implemented meetings that stop 5 or 10 minutes before the hour—creating a natural de-intensification of the workday.

- **Strategy 10: Take a searching look as to where you might be encouraging performative work.** One executive described to me having to go by his direct reports' offices every night to say, "Okay! Let's finish up whatever we're working on at home!" to keep them from feeling like they had to stay late. It's worth auditing everything you do to make sure you're not unconsciously egging on performative work, either through your own behavior or through what you reward. Are you giving higher performance ratings to people who schedule meaningless meetings to show off? Are you over-reporting to your own bosses? It's often striking how much performative work can be stopped simply through one individual in a leadership role calling out their own counterproductive behaviors.

Vetting your organization and your team for intensified, misunderstood, and performative work—and then addressing those problematic work types—can go a long way toward resolving longstanding "glitches" in organizational and team performance. Even beginning a conversation using this language can provide an immediate morale lift—you're putting words to long-held feelings.

Right now, you're probably wondering, though—where did all of this problematic work *come from*? Did this all just happen? The answer is no—there are a couple of villains out there screwing things up for the rest of us, and a whole machine fueling their insidious efforts. In the next chapter, we'll meet these villains, and encounter the machine dragging the future of work back into the past.

2 The Anxiety Monster and the Boss Baby Customer

Slaying Work's Monsters

Having read the prior chapter, you might be thinking right now: gosh, work is a bit of a mess. Haven't folks tried to fix all of this?

Absolutely they have. But it's not as easy as it looks. I learned that very early in my career—join me in the way-back machine to 1997. The country was listening to sprightly hits like "Barbie Girl" by Aqua and "Tubthumping" by Chumbawumba and sporting low-rise jeans [*shiver!*].

And I was 19: curious, ambitious, bumbling, and deeply, deeply clueless. My parents were doctors, so the business world was a mystery. I did suspect you had to do good internships to secure a decent job after college, so I'd gotten my hands on "America's Top 100 Internships" and applied to all of the ones in New York City.

When I got to my summer 1997 internship, at the New York City offices of TBWA Chiat/Day, something inside of me lit up. The famed ad agency ran their East Coast operations from a pioneering open plan environment with zero assigned seats and the craziest

interior design ever. My most vivid memory is of a wall covered in
multicolored fur (presumably synthetic), but historical photos show
gymnasium-style floors with faux graffiti, a mirror framed by Rolling-
Stones-ish lips, and another multicolored wall fashioned entirely
of pillows.

I felt like Dorothy Gale stepping into the vivid land of Oz after a
lifetime in sepia-tinted Kansas. Maybe work didn't have to be boring!
Maybe work could be fun!

In fact, the 1997 TBWA Chiat/Day office was a famous
experiment in changing how we work. Along with their LA office,
which pioneered the concept, it was an early example of hotdesking.
Conceptually, everyone came in each morning, stashed their personal
effects in a locker, and chose what seat would suit them that day.
Would it be a quiet corner by the panoramic windows, overlooking
the tip of Manhattan? Or would it be a tiny desk on what they called
the "trading floor," a big open room actually more reminiscent of an
elementary school classroom than any place stocks and bonds ever
changed hands? The choice was yours, daily.

Except no one, but no one, seemed to actually choose a new desk
every day.

Market research folks had too many paper files to move around
every day, so the group had quietly colonized a back corner of a side
alley and set up permanent shop. The Absolut account team (the
sponsors of our internship project, as well as the purveyors of the
iconic bottles that I later learned were stashed liberally throughout
lockers and desks) had done the same thing, but due to their clout
within the agency were allowed to openly take over an entire room.
Creatives (the folks who write the ads and the top of the agency food
chain) were picky about their spaces, so they weren't going to move
around like nomads if they found spaces they liked.

Worse yet, per a fairly scathing *Wired* article from 1999,[1] the
office I'd been so thrilled to intern in was the last gasp of a failed

experiment that had been detested by workers on both coasts from the very beginning. The office of the future hadn't just stopped working; it had never worked.

For me, that summer many years ago planted a seed of skepticism in my brain about the very idea of "the future of work." Don't get me wrong—that office was cool as heck, and I'd still love to work in a place that looks like an Andy Warhol acid trip (see Figure 2.1).

But seeing the contrast between the lofty vision of the fluid, hotdesked office environment and the actual ways of working for teams that had to get things done every day—it both got me excited about there might be a better way to do this. . .and immediately skeptical about all of the tactics that get deployed.

Which brings us to the theme of this chapter: What's stopping us from making work better? Why don't we do a better job of digging into the experience of work and fixing it? We'll look at two monsters

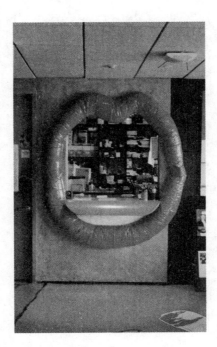

Figure 2.1   TBWA Chiat Day office, 1990s

menacing the world of work: the Work Anxiety Monster and the Boss Baby Customer And then we'll examine the "Workforce Copy Machine" of structures and processes that keeps their efforts going.

"Get Moving Now!": The Work Anxiety Monster

I'd like to introduce you to a character scarier than any horror movie villain you've ever encountered. It's the Work Anxiety Monster. It's in us all, and it's in every organization.

Any student of psychology will tell you that a serious impediment to human happiness and success is the negative stories we sometimes tell ourselves. We run into a friend who's rushing somewhere and think that because he couldn't talk for long, he must be getting bored with our friendship. Kid has a stomachache? Must be a catastrophic illness. And so on. For many people, cognitive behavioral therapy is incredibly helpful fighting depression and anxiety because it causes them to tackle these negative stories and rewrite them into more realistic, constructive narratives. ("Larry must have been in a hurry! I know he has a demanding job," or "Little Susie probably just ate her spaghetti too fast, just like the last three times.")

The problem in organizations is that our individually strange storytelling about work (which follows two set paths that we'll discuss in a moment) adds up to *organization-level* warped narratives—think of a pyramid of cheerleaders. Those catastrophizing stories form a collective anxiety monster that constantly demands to be fed—and contorts the work experience into a Kafka-esque parade of irritating moments. Flawed, anxious thinking gets baked into everything from organizational design to individual processes to workforce decisions from large populations to individual hiring.

The Work Anxiety Monster is effective in part because is only has two simple, interrelated themes, which it repeats over and over to devastating effect: **people are lazy, and people are slow.** On those two misdirected assumptions about human behavior are founded millions of lousy days at work. The issue is not that every manager explicitly believes those things—the issue is that enough have over the years that we've built companies to correct for them—and thus many facets of organizations over-rotate on trying to correct for these problems. This isn't a wholly new idea. Douglas McGregor in 1960 wrote about "Theory X" versus "Theory Y" management,[2] which describes, effectively, assuming folks are self-centered, resistant, and unmotivated versus self-driven, creative, and responsibility-seeking. In my view, though, McGregor's work didn't go far enough—he still admitted the possibility that some workers were not "mature enough" to be seen as "Theory Y workers."

That's the Work Anxiety Monster talking. And in fact, the notion that *some* people are lazy and *some* people are slow drives many of the worst organizational decisions (and showcases a DEI failure when you write it in terms that stark).

Some version of the Work Anxiety Monster has likely been around throughout human history. But it's a safe bet that both the Industrial Revolution and a more global way of working escalated the Work Anxiety Monster's nefarious efforts. As managers became more removed from work—physically or intellectually—their ruminating brains filled in what they couldn't see about their direct reports' day-to-day work with those two anxious messages: "People are lazy! People are slow!"

In fact, at times when work is changing dramatically, people may *look* like they are lazy and slow. I taught myself to fix a toilet recently—replaced the entire innards of the darn thing. A professional plumber would have done the work in a tiny fraction of the time it took me, but also would have looked more expedient doing it too. My brain needed to process the learning in real time and work on the problems that were coming up, so I kept wandering off to get snacks, answer emails, etc. I wasn't being lazy or slow—this was a natural way of working on something novel.

What's interesting about contemporary work—physical work and knowledge work alike—is that across many jobs, the nature of work changes so fast that the folks doing it find themselves repeatedly new to it and thus appear lazy/slow. The Pew Center cites a dramatic escalation in social and analytical skills required across many professions[3] in the 35-year period from 1980 to 2015 (83% greater need, and 77% greater need, respectively). That's a complete sea-change in one person's lifetime. During the COVID-19 period, that already high rate of change accelerated dramatically, as entire workforces shifted from in-person to virtual work, learned to do tasks with sparser personnel, and in general reconfigured work on the fly due to ever-shifting health and safety concerns. This ever-quickening rate of change means that we are, in some ways, as my gamer daughter would say, eternal "noobs"—chronically visibly new to the game we're playing. . .and looking artificially slow and lazy as a result. Figure 2.2 shows some Mercer data on the changing face of skills.

What skills are expected to be the most important to your organization over the next 3 years?

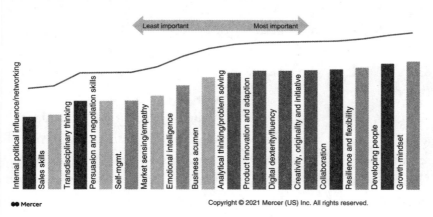

Figure 2.2   The changing face of skills

Source: Mercer LLC.

What are the impacts of designing work for people you believe, on some deeper level, to be lazy and slow? Let's start at organizational level. Believing people to be slow drives work intensification, as the "faster, faster" exhortation gets built into every task and every job. Believing people to be lazy also creates intensified work, as leadership requires more proof that work is getting done—generating extra documentation/reporting tasks for workers or necessitating monitoring that has the same effect. On a team level, these beliefs also increase the proportion of performative work, as workers are constantly given cues that they need to *show* their leaders that they're not lazy and slow.

The Work Anxiety Monster is a menace. But it's not operating alone.

The Taskmaster Boss Hiding Around the Corner: The Boss Baby Customer

Making customers happy is a noble goal, right? A win for both the folks buying your products or using your services, and for the organization itself, which snaps up all of that additional revenue from happy customers buying more products or using more services. We love to talk about "customer centricity" or "customer obsession," even as most folks using those terms haven't the slightest clue what they actually mean. (Right up there with "digital transformation" on the list of words that sound great, but might as well be random grunts for how well they are generally understood.)

At its root, customer obsession should not be a bad thing. In a perfect world, a customer-obsessed organization would empathically look through a customer's eyes, and eliminate any friction that slows or blocks a customer purchase. This includes everything from customers having to look for 2 seconds for a button on a mobile site to how your brick-and-mortar store smells (just good enough for people to stay in it, but not so good that it distracts them from buying things!). In theory, happy customers and happy organizations result.

But in practice, customer obsession has been taken too far—creating "Boss Baby" Customers—who directly or indirectly torment employees. As in the 2017 film, where a suit-wearing baby issues commands to the adults around him, customers have been conditioned in recent decades to be both somewhat helpless (the "baby" part) and totally in charge (the "boss" part). The deep roots of boss baby creation likely lie during the dot-com era, where early e-commerce providers got waaaaaay over their skis, promising the moon to doe-eyed internet newbies. Today, in the COVID-19 era of all home delivery all the time, companies like Buyk and Jokr now promise delivery of basic groceries in **15** minutes, straight from a local bodega-turned-tiny-warehouse (Figure 2.3). We've been conditioned to expect our online orders to arrive in less than a week, often 1 or 2 days. We're often promised remarkable levels of customization or personalization—a favorite clothing company of mine, eShakti, lets you edit dresses, picking your sleeve length or hemline.

Figure 2.3   Bike delivery person
Source: Surprising_Shots / Pixabay.

Eliminating all friction for customers would be wonderful if it could be accomplished through technology. There are two problems with this, though:

- The tech is never as seamless or frictionless as it's supposed to be.
- Even if it was, the physical world is involved too.

Let's walk through a simplified example to see the various points of failure—and how employees then feel the impact.

A customer—we'll call her "Karen"—orders a navy blue t-shirt from a mobile site. The online interface is smooth and quick, and the whole transaction takes less than 5 minutes. The site even promises 2-day shipping, as a promotion for new customers. What Karen doesn't know, though, is that the system she placed the order in is *not* the system that prompts warehouse workers to pack the actual t-shirt. The customer-facing system has to "talk" to the warehouse system, and because some codes pertaining to shirt colors haven't been updated, the warehouse system gets told to pack a white shirt instead. Due to the 2-day shipping goal, a quality control step where employees visually review the packed product has been cut—so the white shirt gets shipped off to the customer.

When Karen gets the wrong shirt, she calls the site angrily—and because customer service is overwhelmed with similar problems (she's not the only one who got the wrong shirt!), she has to wait 10 minutes to talk to someone. She's now waited on the phone twice as long as it took her to buy the shirt itself, and by the time she gets on the line with a customer service rep, she's gone from angry to furious. Let's just say the customer service rep doesn't have such a great time on the phone with her. The rep then contacts the warehouse to get the right shirt sent—amidst a flurry of orders that have to be re-done. Because the "customer-obsessed" organization has

committed to a quick turn on getting the orders right, by the time
the customer service folks have gotten the necessary overrides into a
third system (not the one that handled the customer order or the one
that packed the wrong shirt), warehouse workers have to work at a
faster pace than they can generally handle to get the correct
shirts out.

Now you could say that better tech would have solved many of
these problems—and you'd be right to say that. But we're in a tricky
age: the Age of Iffy Tech. Fifty years ago, say, tech was visibly clunky.
My mom used to scare me with stories of using early computers,
which some office wag had programmed to print out a picture of
Alfred E Neuman inscribed, "It's a Mad, Mad, Mad World," every
time an error was generated. Apparently printing these pictures—
which took hours—was most of what the computers ended up doing.
That was the past of technology, and it was no fun. Conversely, if we
flash forward 50 years in the future, it's not hard to see a smoother
tech-enabled experience, with technology that's far more cognitively
adept and physically nimble.

But unfortunately, we live right now. Right now is the painful
middle distance between the Flintstones and the Jetsons. Right now
technology is great sometimes and downright awful others. . .but we
generally plan on it being great and make promises to Boss Baby
Customers on the basis of tech being great. We also discount the
physical world, which has natural disruptions and limitations. A
delivery app's software can elaborately track the progress of a driver
from a restaurant to a house, but no software in the world can make
it stop raining during that drive. A warehouse's software can monitor
how fast boxes are getting packed, but it can't move workers' arms
faster. And so on.

Someday customers might get to be Boss Babies. But that day
isn't here yet, and we've got to rein things in in the interim.

What to Do: Five Strategies for Organizations

Now that we've met two monsters of the workplace—the Work Anxiety Monster and the Boss Baby Customer—what can we do at an organizational level to start to win back the workplace kingdom? Here are five strategies organizations can use to change their assumptions and get work done less neurotically.

- **Strategy 11: Unpack your foundational talent management assumptions—what decisions have you made on the basis of believing folks are lazy or slow?** You may be staring at the book in horror right now, saying, "We love our employees! We've never made a decision based on the belief that they were lazy or slow!" This is a moment to go on an anxiety monster hunt—digging deep into the implicit assumptions behind your talent decisions. For instance, to what extent do you monitor employees, and critically, *why* do you monitor employees? Are your underlying goals to better understand how to enable them, or are you simply trying to drive compliance with a certain pace of work? Even organizational structure may show the fingerprints of the anxiety monster—it's worth looking for roles or groups that are designed to urge other workers to work harder or go faster. Framed improperly, the best-intentioned Continuous Improvement or Project Management groups can find themselves in this unfortunate role.

- **Strategy 12: Regularly examine the jobs that impact your organization the most—have they changed in a way that affects how people's performance of those jobs looks (i.e., do they look lazy or slow because work is changing fast?)?** We talk a lot about how work is changing, but on the ground in organizations we rarely take a step back and actually measure and take action on that change. Everyone mocks job descriptions—and sometimes they're antiquated and terrible—but they're just an on-paper version of our generally out-of-date thinking about how any job gets done. We need to get into the rigor of *regularly thinking about how work gets done*. Rather than assuming people are doing something wrong, anytime your organization experiences a disruption in a particular role or company segment, look to the work. Are you asking people to do the right things in the right way? Don't be afraid to dig in at a very basic level and to jettison your assumptions. Remember, firefighters spend most of their time not fighting fires, and healthcare workers at times spend more time with electronic medical records than with patients. Work looks different than you'd expect—so keep looking at it!

- **Strategy 13: Map how your customer experience and your employee experience interact. Each time you change your customer experience, how is employee experience impacted? What trade-offs are okay, and which ones are not?** Many organizations map customers' experiences, using different customer personas; similarly, many organizations map employees' experience, again tracing how different personas might interact with the company throughout their life cycle as workers. Few organizations ever look at the two journeys together and how they intersect. It's important to do so not just for your employees, but for your customers as well—think about the impact on a customer if they, for instance, interact with an employee who's been onboarded poorly. For employees, though, this is critical—something as simple as number of days to delivery or number of customizations possible on a product or service can have huge implications to the intensification of their work. This is why your local brunch place doesn't let you make substitutions in your omelet—changing out Swiss for cheddar cheese isn't a simple reach to a different part of the fridge, like it might be in your home kitchen. Your cheese change means everything from how ingredients are organized to how the line cooks perform their jobs might have to shift—creating friction at the kitchen's busiest time.

- **Strategy 14: Tread carefully in how you talk about seamlessness and frictionlessness—internally and externally.** A frictionless experience for customers or employees is a wonderful aspirational goal, but being thoughtful about how you portray how that will play out in reality can subtly but powerfully recalibrate expectations to a place that better serves all of your stakeholders. In particular, arming employees with language to address when things go wrong sends a critical message: the world isn't always going to be perfect, and we don't expect the humans we employ to heroically make it so. Feeling like you can solve for and speak about road bumps destroys the unreasonable power of the boss baby customer.

- **Strategy 15: Actively promote replacements for the Work Anxiety Monster and the Boss Baby Customer.** Align your executive team around what you truly do believe about your employees and your customers—and then play out how those beliefs are or are not reflected in your team's actions. Attacking these corporate villains head on, and consciously articulating a different view of the world, gives the organization a new template for action. Quantitatively and qualitatively framing employee and customer personas can be very helpful here, as a specific vision of behaviors goes a long way toward replacing amorphous anxious feelings that can lead you in the wrong direction in how decisions are managed.

What to Do: Five Strategies for Teams

The impacts of the Work Anxiety Monster and the Boss Baby Customer can be incredibly personal—they can feel like they're inside your own head! While this makes these forces tough to fight, it does mean that they can be confronted day to day, at a team level. Examining your feelings in this regard—especially your own feelings about how *you* work—can feel difficult, but it's worth fighting through your personal resistance to get to a saner view of how you and your team can perform without these malign influences driving unhealthy work.

- **Strategy 16: Examine your feelings about your team—are you seeing them through a Work Anxiety Monster lens? What would you do differently if you didn't assume laziness or slowness?** Here again, you may be protesting as you read this. "I believe in my team! I don't think they're lazy or slow." But test for your deep-down beliefs—the ones you're not admitting to yourself. Every time you say to yourself, "Why can't they just [do whatever it is you want them to do in the time you want them to do it]?" you're dancing with the anxiety monster. Take a step back and visualize what it would be like to have complete trust in your people to get it right in a time frame that will ultimately work for the business. What would you change? Would you send fewer emails? Kill off a pipeline call? Distribute work differently?

- **Strategy 17: Talk to your team about pace—why are you moving at the speed you're moving? What should go faster and critically—where are you going to "slow down to speed up"?** That old UPS tagline about "moving at the speed of business" always makes me think: What is the speed of business? For my whole career it's seemed that we had one speed—faster and faster. But if we're going to shake off the pernicious influences of the anxiety monster and the boss baby customer, we're going to need to start talking about pace—and stop taking "as fast as possible" for granted. Think about how it feels to move really fast in your personal life—how many times have you rushed out the door and left something critical behind? (Best-case scenario being your car keys I guess. . .gets you rushing right back.) We know there's a speed/quality trade-off in life, but we ignore it at work. Having a sensible conversation with your team about when the pace feels off—and when moving faster on tasks *isn't* actually generating faster results—can generate a host of ideas that will, ironically, likely get everything running better and faster in the end.

- **Strategy 18: Examine whether you're inflicting anxiety monster thoughts on yourself. How often are you telling yourself, "I'm lazy, I'm slow"?** I was explaining some of these ideas in this book to a dear friend recently—we've known each other for almost 30 years. When I got to the part about how we needed to stop assuming workers were lazy or slow, she stopped me: "But I'm lazy and slow sometimes!" I couldn't believe my brilliant, capable friend—who does a responsible job for a high-profile organization—would speak about herself that way. In some ways, this is the scariest handiwork of the Work Anxiety Monster: we're at the point of *telling ourselves* that we're lazy and slow. No one externally has to even imply it anymore. I do this to myself dozens of times a day! To get to a better way of working, we have to stop gaslighting *ourselves*—see yourself as someone who does work the right way in the right time, and you'll begin treating others with similar respect.

- **Strategy 19: Talk to your team about their experience of your customer—whether they are customer facing or not! How do they see your customer?** A few former and current coworkers of mine have told me the same joke over the years: "This would be a great business, if it wasn't for the clients." The joke is of course that there would be no business if it weren't for the clients. . .but as the Russian saying goes, in every joke there's a little joke. The fundamental truth in that particular quip is that many, many workers go through their whole careers somewhere between slightly frustrated with and deeply angry at the customer. You don't have to be customer-facing to have thoughts and feelings about customers, either; probe the experiences of folks everywhere from back offices to factory front lines, and they will often paint a detailed picture of the customer that will surprise you—for better and for worse.

- **Strategy 20: Create a team mechanism for calling out appearances of the Work Anxiety Monster and the Boss Baby Customer.** These workplace villains are effective, in part, because they're sneaky: they creep back in despite our best intentions. Teams can combat this by having a mechanism for calling out when things start to go off the rails, either through assumptions that are too dark about their own speed and diligence, or too aggressive about pleasing customers. In consulting, I've often heard folks joke about hiring "insecure overachievers"—the goal here is to dial the insecurity and the overachieving down to levels that are effective and not ultimately self-destructive.

Why Don't Things Get Better? The Organizational Copy Machine

The Work Anxiety Monster and the Boss Baby Customer are dangerous workplace forces, but like any good villains, they wouldn't be successful without a powerful machine helping them. In this case, the organizational machinery that replicates the same ways of working, over and over and over.

We can call it the organizational "Workforce Copy Machine"—the combination of structures and processes that keep us in unproductive, unhealthy working grooves. There are many high-minded theories about why transformations fail, but sadly in the space of work, it's the banal copy machine pursuing sameness with far more energy and resources than anyone has available to pursue differentness. Transformations aren't getting hamstrung by giant boulders in the road; it's subtle sand in the engine wearing them down.

What's in the organizational Workforce Copy Machine that's so destructive to work actually changing in the ways it needs to? Four things:

- Jobs and pay are inextricably conflated.
- Talent acquisition is set up to clone current jobs and people.
- The complexity of the overall system is too high compared to the systems set up to deal with the people side.
- Leadership is rewarded for sameness.

Let's examine each in turn.

Jobs and Pay Are Inextricably Conflated

When organizations do reconsider "ordinary" jobs, it's generally because something is going wrong on the pay front. Maybe people are doing similar jobs for different pay; maybe people have to get promoted to get paid at market rate for their role. It can be hard to get compensation right for in-demand roles, such as data scientists, and this problem triggers a million fairly superficial rethinks of the job itself.

From a pay perspective, it's not wrong to speak about pay and work in the same breath. But the "two-headed monster" of work and pay does work itself a disservice. Paying workers is a massive income statement item—50% or more of gross revenues, per some estimates—and thus becomes a battleship too large to turn quickly. It also becomes a big, fat, cost-cutting target, thus driving a great deal of energy toward reinventing work in the direction of efficiency only, a flat lens that takes current reality and seeks to simply add a few minus signs.

If someone said to you that your paycheck was your job, you'd think that was pretty silly, right? In our intuitive human minds, work and pay sit on two opposite sides of a scale—what you ask me to do, and what you pay me for it. But weirdly, organizations and particularly the HR function smush those two sides of the scale together, and the folks who focus on getting pay right (often the Total Rewards function) look at things like job descriptions off the side of their desk. There's a deep irony here. The main point of an organization, which is people doing work, is completely neglected within its people function. No wonder no one ever rethinks most jobs—while a great deal of interesting thinking and positive change often comes from the Total Rewards function by virtue of terrific individuals there, in practical terms there's *no one to do the full-time work of rethinking jobs!*

Conflating the work of thinking about work and the work of thinking about pay has another chilling effect on innovation in work design: it turns a 3D universe of infinite work possibility into a 2D universe of linear compensation possibility. While the array of rewards and particularly benefits choices has gotten more creative over time, the quantitative universe of rewards is keyed at its root with two directions to go—up or down. This creates a challenging frame for thinking about work, as every change has to trace back to a single impact—does this mean compensation for a job goes higher or lower? Under these conditions, it becomes damn near impossible to "break the frame" on jobs because every rethink toggles quickly back to a spreadsheet.

Talent Acquisition Is Set Up to Clone Current Jobs and People

Another factor impeding a meaningful rethink of work is the clunkiness—and often disconnection—of talent acquisition processes from the coalface where work is performed. Let's say your organization completely rethinks accounting. You figure out a way to do the work totally differently! It's going to revolutionize your financial processes, saving money and time but also creating a fun, creative environment for the folks doing the work. . .all well within the regulatory constraints of your jurisdiction. It's a miracle! And you can retrain many of your folks to work differently, even leveraging some of what they've been doing informally for years.

But. . . . you need to hire a few folks for new roles that didn't exist previously. This is where things get weird. HR probably asks you what job description can be "cloned" for the new role—and since there's not really a precedent for these new roles, you go down a rabbit hole of bureaucracy to simply write something new (and make sure it fits into your organization's existing job structures). Because the set of attributes you might search for are different or in a different combination than prior incarnations of the job, your talent acquisition professionals or search firm then struggle with another version of the "cloning" dilemma—all new and no template to work from. With all new parameters, the whole process moves at a fraction of the speed a standardized talent search would. Once you bring in candidates for the new role, internal evaluators then wrestle with how to evaluate them; they don't have a mental picture of "what good looks like."

The whole system is set up to hire "same." Good luck hiring "different"!

Leadership Is Rewarded for Sameness

Approaches to culture change always emphasize—and rightly so—leadership modeling and supporting the change. But when it comes to work changing, leadership at many organizations will struggle with built-in disincentives to even minor disruptions in the work paradigm. One disincentive should be familiar to many of us—in public and private companies alike, executives are generally rewarded for smooth, predictable results. This serves as a disincentive to all kinds of transformations, but especially to anything that seems to change work on a fundamental level. Another disincentive is subtler, but perhaps even stronger: if we change work at lower levels, the work of management changes. Don't get me wrong—management is happy for work to change if that change seems to make their own unmanageable jobs more manageable. Algorithmic management, for instance, is often cited as "taking work off the plates" of overstrapped human managers, even as it increases the burden on workers. But push the scales in the other direction, and managers (many of whom are desperately overloaded themselves) are not keen to pull the trigger on initiatives that may render their job more difficult—or even so different that they become unsuitable for it.

The Complexity of the Overall System Is Too High Compared to the Systems Set Up to Deal with the People Side

Complexity theory holds that the ideal complexity of any given system is roughly equivalent to whatever in the outside world it's trying to grapple with. You don't want to be far more complex than the world around you, and you don't want to be far simpler either. Now, what's happened within many organizations is that the complexity of the organization itself (consider the outside world for these purposes) has far outpaced either the complexity of human resources or the systems (in a technological and process sense) human resources has set up to deal with people. This could manifest in a number of ways, anything from a single HR business partner facing off against a multi-thousand-person division to a job architecture struggling under the weight of dozens of new roles in emerging areas. In many ways, this phenomenon results from decades of underinvestment in the human resources function, but it's also an outgrowth of the same thinking that drove that underinvestment—the false belief that people issues are not complex.

The bad news about the Workforce Copy Machine is that all of these factors mean it's deeply entrenched. The good news is that doesn't mean it's not breakable. In the next chapter, we'll look at how to break it.

3 Breaking the Workforce Copy Machine

Switching Off the Past, Switching on the Future

"Each time history repeats itself, the price goes up."

—Historian Ronald Wright, quoting a graffiti slogan

Sigmund Freud famously wrote that left to our own devices, human beings will repeat the past—especially the traumatic past—over and over.

As we discussed in the last chapter, organizations have a bit of the same problem—a "Workforce Copy Machine" that quietly, impersonally fights attempts to change and keeps those companies stuck in the same behaviors. . .over and over and over.

With full credit to our CEO, Martine Ferland, who always challenges us to "break the machine" and get Mercer to work better, this chapter takes on the challenge of breaking the Workforce Copy Machine. How do we—at organization and team level—disrupt the forces that unintentionally keep us stuck? How can we create alternate pathways to a future that actually looks different—one that's truly discontinuous from the bad patterns of the past?

In this chapter, we'll first examine how we got into this rut—the strangely dark history of managing people within organizations. We'll then examine a pathway to intentional work, addressing the four trouble spots we talked about in the prior chapter (conflation of jobs and pay, talent acquisition set up to produce "clones," imbalance of complexity in people versus organizational systems, and leadership being rewarded for sameness). Much as better leadership as individuals often entails shutting down pathological behaviors and replacing them with new, healthy ones, better functioning as an organization means demolishing unintentional loops of unintended ways of work, and instituting the choices you'd make *were you intentionally choosing*. And finally, we'll dig into how different the long-static human resources function can and should finally step up to be a strategic engine for the entire organization.

The History of Human Resources Is Dark and Boring

The human resources (HR) function was born more than 120 years ago, during a violent period of clash between labor and management.

In key structural ways, it hasn't changed much since then.

We've sent people into space, weathered two global pandemics, fought countless wars, and developed innumerable technologies, but how we manage people at work, the place most adults spend most of their time, remains remarkably static. HR and the associated people management systems remain a time capsule of the early twentieth century. No wonder "Workforce Copy Machine" organizations keep repeating the past; everything about how they manage people is mired in the practices of a century ago.

This is not to say things haven't gotten better since the Industrial Revolution. Before HR came onto the scene, the imbalance of power between management and workers was, to put it mildly, extreme.

As academic Bradley Rubin noted in the 1970s, "The official use of violence against dissatisfied workers has been frequent and severe in American history."[1] Most experts agree HR was born in a formal sense around the end of the nineteenth century, as organizations finally registered the fact that the dangerous working conditions of the early industrial age might not be the best way to do business. Early HR functions—"welfare secretaries"—were set up to protect the most vulnerable workers, specifically women and girls.[2]

The notion of worker protection sounds quite progressive until you dig into the details of how it got implemented. Much of the framing thinking was explicitly paternalistic, viewing workers as dependent children who had to be saved from their own worst impulses. Companies then acted as harsh parents when these populations didn't behave as they desired. Rubin shares one such anecdote:

> Tolman praised the Colorado Fuel and Iron Company's housing policy, describing it as "a practical and intelligent manner toward bettering the condition of the vast army of people dependent on its various enterprises for support." (In 1914 the CFI evicted the striking miners from their homes and burned down the strikers' tent colony in the infamous Ludlow massacre.)[3]

Yikes.

In fact, the early twentieth century was a crucible of labor unrest. In succeeding years, SHRM researchers note[4] two iconic events take place: the bombing of the *LA Times* in 1910 during a strike, and the infamous Triangle Shirtwaist Factory fire in 1911. There's an interesting tension in the proximity of these events: even as companies were launching a violent response to the burgeoning union movement, events such as the fire (which killed 146 women and girls, who'd been locked in to prevent theft) were dramatically making the case for a paradigm shift in how workers were treated (see Figure 3.1).

Around the same time, the first HR departments emerge. And while we're not going to go down a rabbit hole around the rise of the

Figure 3.1 *LA Times* **bombing**

Source: Unknown author / Wikimedia Commons / Public Domain.

labor movement (we're interested here in what companies did to try to solve the problem of worker happiness *themselves*), it's important to pause and consider the fact that HR sprung up to address a world of work that was quite troubled. Why does that matter? Because diagnostically, part of what troubles HR departments to this day may be this heritage—a "hangover" of long-ago ham-handed management practices from the era of the function's invention. In fact, the direct trigger for the founding of what's believed to be the first HR department—at the National Cash Register Company in 1901—was what Fast Company characterized as a "bitter" strike.[5] To ward off another such labor event, the company established a "personnel" department, focused on "recordkeeping, workplace safety, wage management, and employee grievances."[6]

That list sounds kind of familiar, doesn't it? It's 120 years later, and HR is not that different. Recordkeeping is now HR information systems. Wage management is modern rewards. Employee grievances are now employee relations. Many companies have handed off health and safety to a separate entity, but elements like workers' compensation for on-the-job injuries remain squarely within the HR function.

What this reflects is more than a hundred years of things not changing. The first book written about HR, E. Wight Bakke's 1958 *The Human Resources Function,* is one hugely entertaining example of how consistently HR has been framed over the decades (see Figure 3.2).

Bakke's short monograph could have been published today. His goal is to explain HR to a group that we might today call "haters." Bakke does an eerily perfect impression of the hard-bitten anti-HR crowd: "I don't want to have anything to do with all this damned human resources nonsense. It's about time we learned work is work. It's not management's job to play nursemaid. Their job is to tell folks they hire what to do and how to do it, and when you've paid a fellow for the work he's done for you, that's that." Some version of this lecture echoes through an organization's halls every day; Bakke wasn't describing a problem we left behind in the 1950s.

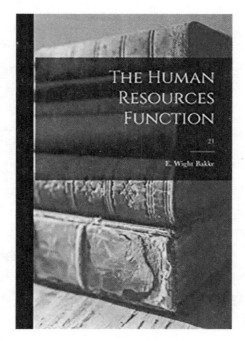

Figure 3.2 *The Human Resources Function,* **by E. Wight Bakke**
Source: Creative Media Partners.

In Bakke's view, organizations have six things to manage: money, materials, people, ideas, market, "and in some cases, nature." He notes that while each other resource has a department logically associated with it (money/finance, materials/engineering, ideas/research and development, market/marketing. . .and nature/conservation, perhaps an environmental, social, and governance predecessor?), people as a resource to be managed needs its own department: HR. As he notes, "Attention to human resources is required not because managers are humanitarians, but because they are managers." In a way, that would resonate for many contemporary organizations, but it stands in frank opposition to much of what we've learned in recent years. Bakke makes it clear that HR is *not* here to make workers happy: "The chief and central concern of the human resources function is not personal happiness, but *productive work*."

Reading *The Human Resources Function* made me sigh—and it made me question why our beliefs and structures have changed so little in more than 60 years, and indeed in the more than 120 years since HR was invented. Examining the data—from Mercer and others—began to produce answers.

Data Tells Us HR Is Starving, Misdirected, and Overloaded

For decades, and across hundreds of organizations, Mercer has examined how HR organizations allocate their time and resources using a proprietary tool called Operations Scanner™. Operations Scanner looks at HR organizations through two lenses. The first, Time Allocation, is a time-and-motion study that enables organizations to understand how their HR function time and labor costs are being allocated using a multidimensional analysis approach. We examine more than 400 activities and link them to factors like function, role, and job level. The second component of Operations Scanner, the Value and Effectiveness survey, is a perception-based survey that allows organizations to elicit from business leaders what they value most from HR and where HR is both meeting and falling short of their expectations. Mercer has aggregated benchmark data from both instruments to track trends and changes over time.

When we look at this data, some dispiriting patterns emerge. Prior to 2018, HR organizations spent about 10% of their time on strategic partnering activities. With all of the seismic change that occurred between 2019 and the present, that percentage went up to 13%, which is hardly a quantum leap in strategic partnership between HR and the broader business.

This is a remarkable statistic. For all of the Great Resignation rhetoric about people issues finally coming to the strategic table, the actual time spent by the folks responsible for people issues on strategy didn't move meaningfully. What happened? My colleague, Karen Piercy explains how HR time and energy was rapidly sucked into day-to-day management of the tactical issues surrounding the COVID-19 pandemic: "I think HR has demonstrated its value during the COVID period, but they've demonstrated its value in being able to manage the crisis and deal with operational issues like COVID testing. . .landing a huge chunk of administrative work on its plate." Figure 3.3 shows some Mercer data on how companies rank HR performance versus effectiveness.

Wasn't technology supposed to help with some of this? Well, in many ways technology has done its part: Workday reports 40%

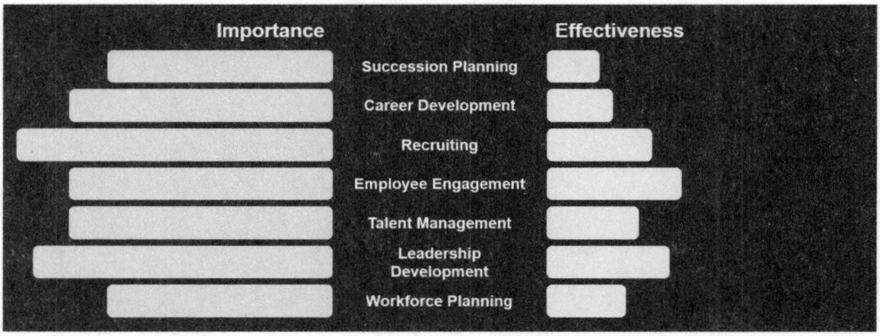

Figure 3.3   How companies rank HR performance versus effectiveness

year-over-year growth, each year, in how many HR transactions their systems handle (https://blog.workday.com/en-us/2021/success-at-scale.html). But human systems and ways of organizing have not kept pace. Our data shows that since 2018, organizations have only experienced a 5% reduction in transacting/recordkeeping. It would seem that we've implemented more technology. . .and then found new transactional activities for humans to perform, instead of moving human labor up the strategic chain.

Our data also show some interesting imbalances in the other activities HR spends time on. Organizations spend roughly three times more time on recruiting new talent versus managing current talent: 20% versus 6%–7%. Workforce data tells us that emphasizing attraction over retention has a negative impact on key areas of economic performance. Studies conducted by our Workforce Strategy and Analytics group show that tenure can be a top driver of performance, trumping other factors; our Marsh colleagues have demonstrated that workers' comp claims spike in association with newly hired employees because those employees are less familiar with safety procedures. Want better-performing employees with a lower cost of risk? Just get the current folks to stick around longer. A diversity lens makes the case for retention over attraction even stronger; the Mercer report "Stepping up for Equity" found that on a data-driven basis, employers seeking to increase representation of Black employees in their populations should focus on retaining the talent they do have, not setting up a revolving door of diverse recruitment but rapid attrition.

Finally, HR remains just plain short on people—in aggregate and in strategically important roles, as well. Data from Saratoga shows the HR function as far more thinly staffed than its peers. Organizations have, at median, one finance employee for every 31 employees and one IT employee for every 28 employees. . .and one HR employee for every 91 employees! That's an effectively threefold difference in investment levels. The picture gets bleaker as you look at strategically important capabilities. Even in the wake of the George Floyd killing and the resulting crisis of conscience across organizations, per data mined from Mercer's Comptryx tool, HR functions employ one diversity/equity/inclusion practitioner per ten thousand employees. Similarly, despite tremendous alleged focus on the need for thoughtful people analytics, the number of actual people deployed against that topic in the HR organization remains minuscule—again, one per ten thousand employees.

We can hardly break the Workforce Copy Machine with HR so stretched, and HR time allocated in many cases so ineffectively. But happily, emergent approaches to rethinking the HR function point the way to a completely different way of operating—to produce a truly different organizational future.

Seizing the Future of HR: Why a Target Interaction Model Is Critical

So let's say your organization wanted to break with the model of the last 120 years and truly do something different with your HR group.

Where would you start?

The dominant HR model of recent decades was invented by Dave Ulrich in 1997. Ulrich proposed a "three-legged stool" wherein HR faced off against employees via shared services, against the business via embedded HR business partners, and against various programs via centers of excellence. Interestingly, as my colleague Karen Piercy notes, Mercer's large-scale research on HR time use shows that while many organizations believe they've implemented this model, their actual structure and use of resources omits at least one leg of the stool, and they would realize meaningful effectiveness gains by simply fully implementing the model they'd already committed to.

In the decades since its invention, the Ulrich model has attracted applause and critique in equal measure. While the implementation of this model has created both efficiency and capability in HR departments around the globe, it has also led HR to operate in ways that shortchange employers and employees alike. My colleague Armin von Rohrscheidt tells the story of a highly skilled engineer at a client organization getting an impersonal call from a shared services center halfway around the world; an entry-level employee reads a script telling him he'll lose his job if he doesn't take an overdue training as soon as possible. From the employee's point of view, the organization seems completely disconnected from the value he provides. From the organization's point of view, this way of operating doesn't make sense either. Would they really fire a highly value-generating employee just because he was a few weeks late on a simple training? It's a failure of both empathy *and* economics.

In an attempt to upend the many disconnects occasioned by the Ulrich model, leading HR experts such as Josh Bersin, Peter Capelli, and Anna Tavis have championed an alternative: Agile HR. Focused on an iterative, real-time approach to everything from coaching to performance management to pay, the Agile movement in HR sought to smash the three-legged Ulrich stool to create kindling for an array of HR engines. Perhaps the most prominent innovation of the Agile HR movement was the creation of Agile pools—groups of HR practitioners who could be deployed against the most urgent or most important tasks at a particular moment in time. Even within Ulrich-structured departments, Agile pools are often deployed today.

Agile pools can be a game-changer for HR departments. Not only can you move resources to the most exigent and important priorities, but offering Agile-pool jobs means you can attract nontraditional talent to HR—curious, versatile individuals who might feel bored or stifled in a more conventional HR role. The trade-off, though, is that organizations that implement Agile pools need to figure out, well, what it is they want those pools of folks to do—in real time, over and over. This requires organizations to have a thoughtful process in place around both near-term and longer-term HR priorities, which sounds like cost of entry in theory, but is not the operational reality of many HR organizations.

At Mercer, we believe that truly reinventing human resources means taking a big step back and not just "zhudzing" the present-day organization. My colleague Armin von Rohrscheidt, our global leader for HR Transformation, uses a funny plumbing analogy to explain:

> *Most of what we do to fix HR today is almost like only changing the faucet. No more water is coming out, or the faucet is dripping, so the organization only changes the faucet. They never change the plumbing—they never solve the root causes of complexity. And going down to the plumbing is what actually frees up resources to create the change you're really looking for.*

To rethink the "plumbing," you can't go straight to a new operating model for HR. It'll be highly theoretical, and it won't be worth the whiteboard it's drawn on! Instead, we believe that, based on their underlying people strategy, organizations should first determine a service portfolio for HR. What should HR do? The answer doesn't have to be the 1901 categories (recordkeeping, pay, employee relations, and health/safety), and it doesn't have to cue off the Urich three-legged stool either. The right answer meets the needs of your organization's people strategy—no more and no less.

The next step is critical: designing a Target Interaction Model for HR. From a design-thinking perspective, this means asking the question, how should different personas within their workforce experience HR? This means asking questions like the following:

What role will the organization's people leaders play?

Will anyone need to shift from business rule enforcers to team coaches? From roadblocks to enablers?

Which interactions should be personal and high-touch?

What key roles are needed to deliver the service portfolio?

What communication channels will be most effective in reaching your workforce?

Do different workforce populations require different types of interactions?

As a part of this design-and-inquiry process, organizations will want to be very thoughtful about which interactions, for whom, should be with human beings and which should be with technological systems—striking a balance of efficiency and empathy. Once a Target Interaction Model is in place, then and only then can a go-forward Target Operating Model for HR be properly constructed, leveraging the insights gleaned as to what service portfolio aspects need to be delivered to whom and how.

Getting the HR model right is critical. But beyond that, organizations can use four key shifts to "break the Workforce Copy Machine" and stop the past from copy-pasting into the future.

Breaking the Four Copy Machine Engines

Some years ago, a book called *Eat This, Not That* was popular. The premise was alluring: you could make simple dietary switches (let's say, hot and sour soup for egg drop soup) and eat a far more healthy diet.

This section is structured in the same vein: Where can you swap out pieces of how your people systems operate to create a healthier way of operating that breaks the copy machine and really changes your organizational future? It's not enough to say, stop doing these things that perpetuate the past—you need something to replace them. Here are four suggested areas of replacement:

From Conflation of Jobs and Pay to Making the Study of Work Someone's Job

Start with a simple question. Is making work better anyone in your organization's job? Probably not. You likely have Total Rewards practitioners looking at job design and architecture, and perhaps Employee Experience practitioners looking at how work is experienced, in certain ways. But work itself is not anyone's job. And that has to change.

Twitter made the switch. They made work someone's job—a focused group of someones. Chief People and Diversity Officer Dalana Brand describes the group:

> We've spun up a whole task force that literally is called Operation: Work. We have cross-functional representation from a variety of different roles in the organization, and the group takes a step back and looks at more effective ways for us to get the work done— increasing collaboration, productivity, innovation. Their job is to take the noise as much as possible out of the system.
>
> —Dalana Brand, Chief People and Diversity Officer

As Brand explains, devoting to focus on work as a sole topic was an outgrowth of learning during the COVID-19 period about how systemic burnout issues needed to be addressed, well, systemically:

> We realized that we need to work differently because people are just tired. They're stressed, they're overworked and having burdensome tools and systems and all that sort of stuff really, really weighs down the people in the organization, which ultimately weighs down our organizational capability and the ability to execute on the things that we need to deliver on. We're thinking about this as a wellbeing journey and really trying to create time and space for our folks to do more meaningful work.

Operation: Work has, to date, taken action on a number of fronts that Brand reports have meaningfully elevated employee satisfaction and productivity alike. Decisions driven by this group have ranged from giving a companywide day off each month and a companywide meeting-free "focus week" each quarter, to culling down the number of communications systems used by employees. In each case, the deciding factor was a simple question: Will this decision make it easier and less burdensome for Twitter employees ("Tweeps" in internal parlance) to get work done?

Virtually every organization would benefit from a similar group. Not every organization can devote resources to it at the level Twitter has, but the model deployed at Twitter has elements that are replicable across an array of organizations:

- The group is focused on making work easier, with the lens that *well employees are more productive*. Everything starts and ends with a business case for employee wellness.

- The group is permanent, not temporary to a crisis period. How work gets done is the very antithesis of a temporary issue.

- The group is cross-functional and brings together a diverse array of thinking. If the study of work comes from a singular lens, you'll generate unidimensional solutions that are imperfect at best. Work is a multidisciplinary topic.

- The group has real funding, true executive sponsorship, and continuous two-way communications with all employees.

From Talent Acquisition That Clones to Talent Acquisition That Questions

A multinational consumer company I once worked with had a fabulous phrase about talent acquisition, referencing the movie *Blade Runner:* "No more replicants." Certainly, no company would *want* to hire the same talent over and over, but due to the factors we've discussed (everything from the difficulty of creating a new requisition from scratch to the sameness biases of hiring managers), many organizations today do, to some extent or another.

How do we flip the switch and create a curiosity-based talent acquisition function? The answer lies in reallocating the energy and resources of talent acquisition far earlier in the process. Today, talent acquisition practitioners often focus their time and effort in executing activities such as sourcing and interviewing while not engaging with the business terribly deeply on more foundational questions, like what truly creates success in a role.

Talent acquisition should serve as a provocateur, constantly seeking to challenge existing beliefs about talent and open up talent pools to less traditional entrants and folks with different capabilities. Ballard Spahr's chief diversity, equity, and inclusion officer, Virginia Essandoh, gives a great example from the legal profession of the unexpectedly diverse array of skill sets needed:

> We have become more much adept at ensuring that we attract and recruit talent across varied backgrounds, perspectives, and skill sets. Workplace culture as well as the needs of clients continue to evolve. We recruit differently than we did 15 years ago, our message is different, our clients' expectations have expanded, and skills and capabilities extend beyond the norm.

What frees up talent acquisition to operate strategically and really challenge talent paradigms? Sensible automation certainly helps, as even in 2022 a good deal of talent acquisition's time is spent on transactional activities, per data from our HR Operations Scanner projects. That said, being thoughtful and careful about user experience is critical. I'll never forget the meeting where a colleague of mine gently informed a client that their link labeled "Click here to learn more about our software engineering jobs" led to a 404 error page. *Oof!*

To avoid generating clones, talent acquisition also needs to be tied to deeper strategic processes around talent. Oftentimes talent acquisition is disconnected from talent assessment (meaning existing capabilities get duplicated and legitimate gaps not filled), strategic workforce planning (meaning actual hiring has nothing to do with what talent the organization believes it needs going forward), or even budgeting processes (meaning finance and HR have periodic showdowns, which is good for neither group).

From a Complexity Mismatch to a Robust People System

Remember those scary staffing ratios from earlier in the chapter? Where HR had, effectively, one-third of the people on a proportional basis that finance or IT did? When it comes to struggling to face off with the complexity of modern organizations, low levels of HR staffing is just the tip of the iceberg. Due to the pace of work and skills change today, many organizations' skills frameworks, career paths, job architectures, succession processes, and other critical people management systems dramatically lag the complexity of actual business operations. You're chasing a clowder of cats with a single butterfly net.

Is the solution to rigorously update every people process your organization has? As a consulting leader, it would be deliciously self-serving for me to offer that as an answer. The real answer, though, is a bit more streamlined: to create a robust, sustainable people system (including but far bigger than HR!) that can deal with current and future complexity, organizations need to put a few critical building blocks in place.

First, truly invest in people analytics, going as high up the analysis chain as is appropriate to your ability to invest, but starting with capture and management of data on the humans you employ as a nonnegotiable. You may not be able to invest in sophisticated predictive analytics, or even hire analytics personnel, but it is within every organization's reach to capture and record key data about their workforce. Cleaning up simple issues—like using the same shorthand for the same terms consistently or having a single system of record— gets you to data-driven conclusions about your people faster than fancy software that will struggle to do anything with incomplete, ever-multiplying, or mangled data sets.

Second, make sure you are well-centered on your approach to employee listening—based on what's relevant to your business, not what's always been done, or what's trendy. If people analytics gives you the employer-centric view of the organization, employee listening is critical to giving you the employee's-eye view. Similar to analytics, employee listening doesn't have to be incredibly elaborate to be effective—it simply needs to be timely, accurate, and focused on the right people issues. At Mercer, we're putting increasing stock in ethnographic techniques in people listening, such as day reconstruction, where employees are asked to narrate their feelings through the work day, using their calendar as a reference. Knowing how people feel as they do different work can inform far smarter decisions about work, and combining this information with more traditional, larger scale methods such as pulse surveys and digital focus groups can provide a true micro-to-macro, comprehensive view of how your employees see your organization.

Finally, taking into account the evidence-driven picture of your organization you've assembled via smart people analytics and employee listening, identify the few battles you must win, and audit the associated processes based on outcomes, not the processes themselves. For instance, let's say your people data shows attrition of ethnic and racially diverse individuals at executive levels, and your employee listening data shows that ethnic and racially diverse individuals have far lower levels of trust in the organization's career paths than others. Performance management and succession planning are your natural targets, and your diagnostic criteria are twofold: who's not succeeding who should be succeeding, and who's succeeding who should not be? By using evidence to home in on key priorities, you can then build sustainable systems going forward that can grapple with the complexity of the challenges you face.

From Rewarding Leadership for Sameness to Rewarding Leadership for Daring

In the movies, we love a good rebel. Think about the last time you watched a movie where the police force was prominently featured. Was the hero or heroine a police officer who followed every departmental protocol, or was it, all too often, a rogue cop, doing the job their own way? We cheer for these characters, believing their understanding of how to do the important work of policing clearly supersedes that of, well, everyone around them.

In real life, though, people who try to do work differently drive us nuts. You might root for *Die Hard's* John McClane on Sunday night, but if your work buddy decides to practice a rogue version of accounting on Monday morning, you're not going to be too pleased. In the real world of work, we're constrained by everything from regulation to technology to fear of the unknown. Moreover, our personal autopilot makes our jobs doable, day to day; it would be exhausting to reinvent too frequently, and we'd inevitably lose focus on what the end results of our work should look like.

This phenomenon is multiplied when we get to leadership level, where the stakes are highest. When was the last time you heard a C-suite leader or a board member say, "We are seeking maximum volatility in our business!" Yeah. . .me neither. Public company or private, while we often prioritize growth, we want to shoot down the highway with as few jarring bumps as possible. We reward leaders accordingly, often putting into place explicit incentives for predictable results. This gives them little motivation to make change to how work gets done or the workforces that do it. Imagine being a chef who's rewarded not for how good the food tastes, but for minimizing the number of people who get indigestion from your cuisine. Your restaurant is going to be pretty bland!

Worse yet, many organizations pay even their top leaders in vague, amorphous ways that send no message at all, leading leaders to infer whatever they want. My colleague Will Ferguson, a leading thinker in the area of jobs and rewards, explains:

> They have one big blob of pay that they expect will send every
> message possible about behavior. That's impossible. It's just

impossible, it's the recipe for no messages. It's a recipe for make it up yourself.

How do we create incentive systems for executives to reach for a future way of working different from the past? Setting goals or objectives and key results too ambitious to be achieved by an extension of current methods is one strategy; taking a portfolio strategy and by role rewarding some leaders for discontinuity and others for smoother progress is another. Working with executives on their personal anxiety monster is also a viable approach—some fears about new ways of working really do stem from the belief that working populations are slow or lazy.

What to Do: Five Strategies for Organizations

Breaking the Workforce Copy Machine at organization level can feel both arduous and deeply satisfying. When results start coming through—when you're truly hiring different people, deploying them differently, getting them to do different work using different methods—well, the different results can be pretty exciting. But knowing where to start on some of the shifts described in this chapter can be daunting. Here are a few places:

- **Strategy 21: Create a "single account of the truth" on the workforce of your organization—however you employ them—and systems and processes to maintain it in real-time.** Of all of the recommendations in this book, I'll be candid, this is one of the most difficult to implement, requiring focused partnership between HR, procurement, finance, and likely IT. Through the process, be prepared for and cognizant of many states of the world: rather than a black-and-white full-time-employee-versus-contractor breakdown, you'll likely encounter different levels of part-time employment, constructions like temp-to-perm, etc. And this is a good thing, even if it makes your workforce trickier to parse out in the short term (and IT systems challenges exponentially more difficult); it means some level of creativity is being deployed in how work gets done. Form a language to describe the different kinds of employment at your organization, use that language to capture the realities of those populations in dynamic systems. . .and then build go-forward financial benchmarks as to what different kinds of work actually cost and the impact they produce. You can't break the Workforce Copy Machine without a pretty clear account of what "today" actually looks like.

- **Strategy 22: Maintain and periodically energize an organization-wide conversation about how work gets done.** During the COVID-19 period and especially as the Great Resignation heated up, many organizations for the first time spoke honestly about *how* work was getting done—balancing discussions of productivity and burnout, and for the first time, getting into the weeds of topics like how many meetings a day is appropriate. Maintaining this thread of discussion—and periodically really kicking it up a notch—is a key lever in breaking the copy machine. Bad patterns of how work gets done often persist simply because we don't talk about them. We implement tactical, short-term initiatives ("No meeting Fridays!") and then chip away at them over time. . .until their effectiveness has been blunted entirely. Keeping the dialogue open keeps the notion of getting work right in the spotlight—and keeps solutions flowing.

- **Strategy 23: Optimize how work gets done by different populations, tackling one chunk at a time.** In partnership with renowned academic John Boudreau, Ravin Jesuthasan (my colleague and Mercer's Global Transformation leader) has written perceptively and systematically about how deconstructing work down to task level and reconstructing to optimize for who can best perform each task (from automation to full-time employees to gig labor) can meaningfully improve productivity and worker experience. Diving methodically, with single-minded focus, into key roles that are experiencing challenges—such as nursing in healthcare systems— can produce exponential change that ripples across a far broader swath of the organization.

- **Strategy 24: Reinvent HR—on your organization's terms.** Reading about the 1901 or 1958 visions of HR from earlier in the chapter, did things sound a bit too familiar? HR is ripe for reinvention, but reinventing just to reinvent won't break the copy machine. Rethinking HR using a Target Interaction Model— where the function's activities genuinely match different employee groups' needs—yields a function that can push the organization into the future by actually reconciling employer and employee needs rather than simply trying to maintain an uneasy peace between the two groups.

- **Strategy 25: Just do less.** Corporations' internal anxiety monsters push for more and more actions and more and more complexity, in the same way our brains trick us into eating a whole bag of potato chips. You don't need all those chips, and you don't need all those activities either. Less feels good, consistently; more rarely does. Moreover, a crowded environment lets archaic people and practices and ways of working continue to hide out; in a sparser landscape, areas to make change become far more apparent.

What to Do: Five Strategies for Teams

At team level, breaking the Workforce Copy Machine can actually be a lot of fun. Figuring out the ways in which your team does silly things over and over and truly shutting down doing those things feels incredibly freeing. Think of the following as a starter recipe for team happiness!

- **Strategy 26: Figure out your worst patterns—and have an honest conversation on how to break them within your team.** Have a therapeutic moment with your team. What are all of the things you collectively do over and over that are unproductive? What is the team past you'd like to stop living in? Do you swirl and argue in meetings? Do you run off in many directions and only align in moments of crisis? Do you approach problems too conservatively and fret when they don't get solved? Whatever your repeated team behaviors are, diagnosing them and breaking the cycle does an incredible amount to break the Workforce Copy Machine at team level.

- **Strategy 27: Build your replicants—then destroy them.** Similar to the prior strategy, one way to break the cycle of hiring similar talent over and over is to first have an honest conversation among your team about what the "replicant" looks like. Look across demographics, background, professional roots, capabilities: What do you hire for over and over? How much of that repetition is productive, and how much of it is unconscious and often unproductive? And when is unproductive repetition linked to productive repetition, where it would be useful to decouple the two? For instance, you may find that your team has consistent success in hiring ex-military personnel, as many organizations do. But if that focus means you hire 30-something white men over and over and over, it may be worth deeper consideration of your criteria and talent pools, preserving former military as a key hiring population, but widening your demographic lens within that group.

- **Strategy 28: Turn your reasons not to hire into reasons *to* hire.** For years, based on a blog I wrote, I've conducted an exercise with audiences called "The Right People Look Wrong." The audience breaks up into small groups, and each group has to list all of the reasons you wouldn't hire someone. Then you challenge the groups—take each reason not to hire someone, and flip it—why would that mean you *should* hire them? Inevitably, the groups excel at turning each negative into a positive. "Jumpy" resumes, for instance, can mean people are agile and intellectually curious. Less than dynamic interviews can mean people are introverted and thoughtful. And so on. Regularly interrogating all of your hiring assumptions can break the cycle of hiring replicants.

- **Strategy 29: Test and learn on disruptive approaches to getting work done, utilizing team contracts if helpful.** Some of the most interesting progress on creating new ways of working happens at team level. For example, it can be tricky at organizational level to try out approaches like shifting whole swaths of meetings to asynchronous communication, but teams can make the switch with relative ease. During the COVID-19 period, some organizations even began to deploy "team contracts" to allow teams to set optimal ways of working within the team. Codifying new ways of working in writing, and then programmatically measuring their success, can break the Workforce Copy Machine for teams in the near term and organizations in the longer term, as replicable case studies are developed.

- **Strategy 30: Not to sound repetitive, but just do less.** Pruning down an ever-growing array of initiatives isn't just the work of organizations—it's the work of teams, too. At team level, staying heads-down in too many activities can leave leaders and team members alike perpetually on autopilot, and stuck in endless loops of sameness. Breaking the Workforce Copy Machine means creating thinking space—and teams have to do less to have that space. More thinking space equals more innovation, and more innovation equals a host of business wins. Once again, a positive employee experience and underlying economic goals work in congruence and harmony.

Breaking the Workforce Copy Machine, at organization or at team level, is exciting stuff. Once we kick some bad habits, we have space to think and do differently. . .and that's where a new style of human-centered decision-making can enter the picture.

4 Decisions About People, for People

How to Make the Human-Centric Decisions That Drive the Next Generation of Greater Organizational Outcomes

My Grandpa Joe was a plant engineer, and according to family lore (unconfirmed), he invented the machine that makes Tam-Tams, a kind of octagonal matzo snack (Figure 4.1). He was a lifetime union guy—it even says on his tombstone, "A friend of the working man." Because he was so good at matzo machine engineering, he eventually rose from line engineer to management.

And it ruined him. He couldn't mentally shift from his deep and strong identification with the struggle of workers to trying to support the agenda of the company he worked for. He floundered and was laid off. He never consistently worked again.

As I've taken on leadership roles of increasing responsibility in my own career, I've thought about this a lot. Why was it so hard for him to cross that psychological line between worker and company? And thinking about the same problem in reverse, why do companies wrestle so mightily to put themselves empathetically into the minds of their workers? Even in organizations that fervently believe in crossing this divide, we see efforts to do so go awry. Matrix structures

THE B. MANISCHEWITZ CO.

Figure 4.1   An early 20th century Manischewitz factory

Source: Wikipedia, Public Domain.

designed to empower greater swaths of employees tie up those same employees in loops of bureaucracy. Enhanced employee experience becomes a stalking horse for longer work hours, as that delicious cafeteria food subtly traps folks at work past dinnertime. And so on.

At Mercer, as we framed our thinking on workforce transformation, we made a conscious choice to show employer and employee across from each other—a parallel balancing act, not a mountain with employer gazing down at the employees at the bottom. This reflects a deep re-set on vision, and one that's been a long time coming. We've been trying to shake off command-and-control leadership for decades and have been puzzled by how poorly that's gone. I remember vividly a discussion with a colleague at a prior job: I'd put "command and control" on a slide, and they'd laughed and told me that was "very 1970s." I persuaded them to keep the phrase on there, and when we sat down with the client, they pointed right at the phrase and said, "Command and control. That's our problem. You nailed it!" It's funny, both the client and my colleague were right: command and control is very 1970s. . .and it's *still around*. And it's going to persist, unless we can start looking through the dual lens of employer and employee with the two groups eye to eye.

Why is it so crucial to look at business through the lens of both economics *and* empathy? Simply put, we see in the data that making human-centric decisions is a powerful economic engine. For instance, in Mercer's 2022 Global Talent Trends data, we see that the highest-growth organizations are both twice as likely to publicly set standards and targets related to responsible work practice, and twice as likely to provide a fair, transparent and secure working environment for all. There's something beautifully clarifying about thinking about your employees as people and working with their human wants, needs, and foibles rather than trying to contort them into mechanistic ways of working. Work with the way humans work, and a new frontier of productivity and impact is possible. Let's explore how to do so.

A Framework for Making Work Work for People

How do we make work work for people? If we wanted to "do work better"—in a deep and fundamental way—how can we point the ship in a different direction? The answer lies in a better framework for decision-making about work, reorienting the seemingly prosaic choices we make about work with a completely shifted lens. We have to tell the anxiety monster to shut up, but we also have to replace its nagging voice with a different voice entirely: a voice that doesn't tell us all to "suck it up" and quietly suffer through the many aspects of work that have been broken for so long. The new voice shaping work decisions balances empathy (a deep respect for workers as fellow human beings) and economics (a pragmatic sense of the business world). Here's a four-point framework for how we can start making human-centric decisions that enable greater sustainable growth and productivity (Figure 4.2):

- *Humanism*: This decision works with how people, and their lives, work—enhancing business outcomes by creating a more natural flow of work.

- *Inclusion*: This decision enables as many people as possible to do the work—lowering the cost of talent and creating better conditions for innovation through greater diversity.

- *Realism*: This decision will keep work going without excessive human effort, even if technology and process don't totally work, enhancing business resilience and day-to-day productivity.

- *Sustainability*: This decision allows work to be doable in the long run under changing conditions, creating sustainable business models.

Humanism
This decision works with how people, and their lives, work—enhancing business outcomes by creating a more natural flow of work.

Inclusion
This decision enables as many people as possible to do the work—lowering the cost of talent and creating better conditions for innovation through greater diversity.

Realism
This decision will keep work going without excessive human effort, even if technology and process don't totally work, enhancing business resilience and day-to-day productivity.

Sustainability
This decision allows work to be doable in the long run under changing conditions, creating sustainable business models.

Figure 4.2   A Framework for human-centric decisions

Humanism

We'll start with this element of the framework because it's arguably the hardest to tackle. It shouldn't be hard to treat people like people, but organizations often visibly struggle. For instance, look at the multiplicity of Occupational Safety and Health Administration (OSHA) regulations around things like going to the bathroom. OSHA offers very specific guidance on both bathroom breaks and what the bathroom facilities should look like. For instance, there are designated employee-to-number-of-full-toilet ratios (urinals don't count!), and accommodations must be made for folks with medical conditions who have to go more frequently. Oh, and at work you can't eat in the bathroom. That's both gross in life and officially dubbed as gross by the regulators.

Now, depending on your political stripe, you might say that this is "regulation ad absurdium," in other words, government trying to control the most basic details of the workplace. But think about it—behind every regulation, there's a workplace that went wrong. Someone didn't offer enough toilets. Someone offered really dirty ones. Someone offered toilets, but no place to wash your hands. And someone was out there—at least one someone—not letting workers go to the bathroom at all! It seems completely inhumane. And yet that was happening.

It's still happening. A grim Centers for Disease Control and Prevention (CDC) blog cites professions from poultry workers to bus drivers doing without bathroom breaks.[1] And bathrooms are just the most vivid example of where organizations cut corners on basic human stuff. Ever tried to pump milk for a baby at work? I worked in one workplace where men serially tried to enter the "wellness room," believing it to be stocked with fruit (what a lovely fantasy!); on a work trip, I once pumped in a videoconference room, staring in fear at a camera that periodically threatened to flicker on. In blue-collar workplaces, the stories go from goofy to openly unsafe, as workers are

routinely asked to pump in those same dirty bathrooms—
endangering the lives of the babies the milk is intended for.

Beyond bathrooms and pumping, the issue of sleep showcases
another collision between mainstream working practice and
humanism. Interestingly, sleep is often an issue for the highest paid
workers. The pace and global nature of work at the top of
organizations means that an entire class of workers with very
responsible roles exist in a perpetual state of sleep deficit and jet lag.
I have fond memories of various bosses over the years slumped over
asleep in meetings. They weren't slackers, and with a few exceptions,
most weren't exhausted party animals. They'd just been on calls at
crazy hours, on and off planes for days, etc. Who could blame them
for nodding off?

When it comes to sleep and work, for me it's also personal. For as
long as I can remember, I've been kind of sleepy. I would come home
and nap for 2–3 hours every day in high school. In my 20s, I'd nod
off in cabs in the early evening. As a young consultant, I'd carefully
structure work-from-home days to include some time to doze. It
seemed like I was always a little behind on sleep—a little off,
energy-wise.

When I had my daughter Mira, of course the exhaustion got worse.
I figured this was normal: moms of newborns are supposed to be tired,
right? But as my daughter grew from a fitfully sleeping baby to an
energetic elementary-schooler, I stayed exhausted. Not just tired,
exhausted. Exhaustion is when your brain feels like gelatin, loose and
wobbly; when aches and pains plague your body, physically dragging it
toward the ground; when your emotions swirl like a tiny craft on rocky
seas. That last one is particularly hard in the workplace context—I
ended up wavering and shaking in situations where I should have been
resolute and firm. Worst of all, being exhausted leaves you incredibly
vulnerable to bullying and manipulation. There's a reason why the
Geneva Convention cites sleep deprivation as a form of torture[2]—as

one academic notes, "Forcing a prisoner to remain awake and alert for days at a time can have a dramatic effect on their cognitive ability, and may cause temporary increases in stress, depression, and hallucinations." If you're looking for a coworker to push around, a sleep-deprived one is an easy mark—and I found the already difficult impacts of exhaustion compounded by the predatory behaviors it triggered in others.

Times got tough. I vividly remember a coworker berating me for not wanting to do a 10:30 p.m. call with an APAC client after stepping off a redeye flight that morning. They were apoplectic about how I wasn't showing commitment to the client; I was literally unable to imagine staying up that late that particular day!

I started looking for solutions. Was the issue ADHD, making my brain fuzzy around the edges? No, it turns out, though ADHD meds did, for a time, help literally keep me awake. Was it thyroid problems, common in both women my age and my own family? Nope—tests came back negative. My doctor urged me to keep looking—incredible credit to her, she fought the narrative I'd internalized for so long. It *wasn't* normal for working moms to be so exhausted, she kept telling me.

She was right. A full-on overnight sleep study revealed what had been sapping my life force for most of my life: sleep apnea. Apparently, my tongue falls into my throat and chokes me in my sleep 14 times an hour! This is what's considered a "mild" case of apnea, as defined by number of times you stop breathing but not the severity of impact. Per my sleep doctors, my "somnolence" score—a measure of sleepiness—was high enough that he recommended against driving a car! (Luckily I live in Manhattan and wasn't doing that anyway.)

I got treated for sleep apnea, and my life changed. Thanks to a Mandibular Advancement Device, which forces my jaw into a position where my tongue can't choke me, I now get productive sleep. I'm not dragging from the first moment of the morning. When I wake up, my brain snaps into order. My shoulders don't ache as if I've been carrying a heavy burden all night. I feel an invisible wind at my back all day—that ordinary flow of energy that many folks take for granted their whole lives.

I've seen it firsthand: sleep matters, just like so many biological imperatives we studiously ignore. During the pandemic, researchers at Stanford were able to identify four different ways that back-to-back Zoom meetings actually cause neurological problems: our brains are tormented by the excess up-close eye contact, seeing ourselves on video for too long, reduced mobility as you sit in front of a screen, and general cognitive overload of a video meeting. Collectively, as a society, we were hurting our brains. . .without improved business results to show for it.

How do we inject more humanism into our business decisions so that we don't compromise worker experience and productivity/ impact alike?

First, we remember to shut down the Work Anxiety Monster. We're not dealing with lazy, slow folks here: we're dealing with normal people with normal human needs. Believing in humanism is crucial: as long as you harbor the worry that humanist behavior will cause the system to grind to a screeching halt, it's very hard to implement the often small tweaks (say, placing meetings an hour later in the morning) that create a human-centered workplace.

Then, we apply an ethnographic lens; in simple terms, you follow people around and see what they do.

If you're trying to figure out where humanism is breaking down, you need a tactic—ethnography—that forces the researcher to marinate in the minutiae of the subject's work experience. It's in those little details that humanism critically breaks down—not being able to leave quite early enough to pick up your kid at afterschool, a water fountain just slightly too far away for a construction worker to use on her break, one too many 6 a.m. meetings at a time of year when there's no sunlight until 8 a.m. We need to watch people trying to be people at work—and to understand where we're treating them in a way that's somewhat less than human.

Inclusion

Let's look at inclusion from a slightly different lens than we usually do. We often look at it through the lens of needing a more diverse array of people and thinking to better solve business challenges. And that's the right way to see things, big picture—the business case has been proven over and over. But sadly, we're not making enough progress.

So let's try a different paradigm. Let's think about solving a classic talent acquisition problem—jobs that not enough people are "qualified" for. What happens when talent pools are too small for a given role? Well, as any good talent acquisition specialist will tell you, a few things, all with direct or indirect negative economic implications:

- Jobs take longer to fill.
- You have to pay more for the talent you do hire.
- To fill roles quickly, you may make compromises on talent that you would have previously deemed unacceptable.
- You end up hiring a homogeneous group of people to do certain work.

What's interesting about this classic set of problems is that we rarely try to solve them in a foundational way: by shaping jobs that a larger group of people can do.

Let's take a silly, brute force example to illustrate the problem. Let's take a high-profile role as an example: chief executive officer

(CEO). Per the Bureau of Labor Statistics, the United States has about 200,000 CEOs today.[3]

Now let's make some goofy assumptions. Let's say, for reasons of career progression and retirement age, you believe that CEOs should be between 50 and 59 years old. And let's say you're a snob and think CEOs should have gone to Ivy League colleges.

Ivy League schools graduate about 13,500 folks a year.[4] And let's assume that about 25% of folks die before reaching age 60.[5] So at any time you should have 13,500 people who graduated per year times the 75% survival rate times 10 possible graduation years, which equals 101,250 people.

That's 101,250 people for 200,000 jobs! With a small set of criteria, you're already at half the talent pool you need.

Now of course, that's a crazy example. In real life, only 11% of Fortune 100 CEOs, at least, come from the Ivy League.[6] For this vital job, which can't go unfilled, the "right" talent comes from an array of foundational sources, which is great. But when we look for folks for other roles, we blithely make an array of assumptions that gate off large talent populations from even applying. For instance, 60% of jobs in the United States require a bachelor's degree.[7] Do that many jobs actually require a college education? Likely not. But we've long used the idea of college education as a proxy for deeper evaluation of candidates for a role—a shorthand for some version of "acceptability." Anyone who's spent any time in the diversity, equity, and inclusion space will tell you, the second we go to shorthand and nebulous concepts of "acceptable," bias creeps in with unbelievable speed and force. The "college education" shorthand has an incredibly distorting impact on the workforce. For instance, 10% of college graduates are Black[8] compared to Blacks being 17% of the overall population. For that dimension of diversity, you've reduced your pool by 42%—*before you started looking at candidates.*

College education is, again, a brute force example. There are an array of "gatekeeping" requirements for roles that operate just as strongly, but more perniciously—everything from the inclusion of particular technical skills that might not really be needed, to *not* including particular "soft skills" (such as empathy) that might actually be needed, to focusing on particular colleges and universities for hiring—even up to the very language of job descriptions, which extensive research has shown has differing impacts on men versus women (men are energized by certain language that dissuades women from applying).

Thinking about inclusion in how work is constructed isn't limited to technical criteria for hiring. Consider a couple of aspects we might take for granted in a strategy consulting role: long hours and needing to be a strong presence in meetings. Long hours can be rough for caregivers, who according to one Bank of America study make up nearly half of the workforce.[9] An array of research describes the workforce as 30%–50% introverts.[10] Again, just statistically, you've knocked out at least half to far more than half of the talent pool for the role. You might say, okay, strategy consultants shouldn't be caregivers or introverts. But is that something you actually believe or want to say? Or are those just implicit assumptions that we've gone along with forever on autopilot? Rethinking "what it takes" for a role is a powerful inclusion lever—and to date, a dramatically underutilized one.

After all, as work continues to morph and change, taking away our preconceptions creates space for the people we really need. The roles of the future will require both new skills and an affinity for different kinds of work, and in a climate of labor shortages, we can see how it can be difficult to find both the capability to do the work and the *desire* to do the work in the same person. As long as we look at the same people over and over, finding the right talent for the future will get more and more difficult. Human-centered decision-making with an inclusive lens on talent makes the skills journey far easier, making the economics of new work simply compute better.

Realism

We all enjoy a good kludge. There's a Reddit called "There I Fixed It," featuring things like cars with their bumpers duct-taped on, for a reason (Figure 4.3). But we all do too much of it, and that's part of what wears workers down. As we'll dig into in Chapter 5, the experience of technology at work often grinds workers down. Process fails too. Whatever percentage of humans are naturally great process designers, perhaps twice as many are doing that work, it often seems!

To enhance realism in our decision-making, the technique we'll use here is scenario planning—let's figure out a range of possible failures, then define the if-thens. It can be taboo particularly to talk about possible tech failure (and we'll get into why in Chapter 5), and process failure is often not even considered as a possibility. Actually mapping out where and how things could fail, how badly they could fail, and what the solution's going to look like can take an enormous amount of weight off workers' shoulders.

Figure 4.3   r/thereifixedit

Source: Reddit Inc.

When I started writing this chapter, I was determined to write about Chernobyl. Perfect anecdote right? Tech failure? Check! The reactor melted down. Process failure? Check! All of the fail-safes turned out not to be so fail-safe. People jumping in to save the day? Check! At one point you had workers swimming under a nuclear reactor on fire. Next time you have a bad day at work, ponder that one. Your bad day is generally not as bad as those guys' bad days. It's a pretty epic illustration of what we—unfairly—end up expecting from employees to deal with tech and process failures.

But the more illuminating anecdote is actually a different story from earlier days in the Soviet Union. It's the story of Stanislav Petrov, "the man who saved the world." (See Figure 4.4.) In 1983, Petrov was working as an early warning specialist,[11] just outside of Moscow. His job was to watch a computer for signs of U.S. missile launches. On September 26 of that year, the computer told him something catastrophic: the Cold War had gone hot. Missiles were incoming.

His screen said "zapusk"—"launch."

Technology had given him clear guidance. The associated process was clear—he was to call his supervisors as soon as the alert sounded. But Petrov hesitated and called colleagues to see if satellite data had indicated the presence of missiles. No one had seen anything. Petrov called in a system malfunction instead of reporting the beginning of nuclear war.

The decision ultimately cost him his career (Soviet officials didn't take kindly to someone subverting processes in the missile arena) but also saved millions of lives. There were no U.S. missiles—just a terrifying tech failure.

Petrov's story is an extreme example, but some version of his no-good, awful, very bad day at work happens to pretty much everyone, all of the time. We're constantly asked to stand in between tech and process failures and total disaster. We might not be ignoring phantom

Figure 4.4   Stanislav Petrov

Source: Queery-54 / Wikimedia Commons / CC BY-SA 4.0.

missiles or swimming under radioactive flames, but our human energy and ingenuity is continually tapped to compensate for the breakdown of the things that are supposed to "just work" all around us. And to some extent—fair enough. For now, we're far smarter than any technology, and we'll always be smarter than any process.

But we do ourselves a disservice by *always relying* on human workers to always tape the bumper back to the car, so to speak. If we can take process and especially technology off of the pedestal of invincibility that we've put them on, and plan for failure, we won't get whacked so badly every time things go wrong. That's where scenario planning comes in—let's say the quiet part out loud and admit this new system might not work quite right. Let's be humble and say that our beautifully designed process might have some natural points of failure. And then let's map out what happens then, instead of sapping endless brainpower and energy making workers figure out the kludge. Human-centric decisions take into account the complicated relationship between humans and technology and never leave human beings, and by extension business outcomes, in the lurch.

Sustainability

Ask any company in the world, "Are your workers disposable?" and
only the most dark-hearted ones would respond, "Yes!" Conceptually,
the vast majority of organizations value their talent and, especially in
this time of labor shortages, would like them to stick around for a bit.
But when you examine talent practices and decisions around how
work gets done, the picture glitches out in several ways:

- *Roles designed for obsolescence.* We love early-in-career workers,
  who do a monstrous amount of work for organizations, but we
  don't love to employ them for very long! Across professional and
  financial services, an army of analysts churn out presentations and
  pitchbooks, toiling late into the night fresh out of college.
  Analysts are expected to generate a great deal of fairly mechanical
  output and vamoose back to business school after 2–3 years. It's a
  strange sort of social contract—trading off high-intensity work for
  on-the-job training that ranges from wonderful to terrible (often
  depending more on who your boss is than what massive
  organization you work for), plus credentialing that gets you into
  an MBA program so you can be. . .credentialed to work for a
  similar set of massive organizations. Now, it wouldn't necessarily
  be problematic that these roles are designed to be temporary, but
  their temporary nature is then used to justify large amounts of
  intensified work (think consultants churning 40 versions of a
  document) and performative work (think investment bankers
  staying in the office until 2 a.m. because everyone else is there
  too). In the blue-collar world, as with so many things, the picture
  is similar but worse. Seasonal workers often suffer the worst-
  designed roles, performing terrifyingly intensified round-the-clock
  work during the Christmas rush or the harvest season. Because
  many of these workers are immigrants in the United States on

temporary visas (a topic we'll dive into more deeply in Chapter 7), they literally disappear when these periods of backbreaking work are done (as opposed to the consultants and bankers, who just head off to business school).

- *Physically or mentally overwhelming work.* From picking strawberries to moderating social media interactions, a large number of jobs take a physical or mental toll on workers that cannot be sustained over the long term, regardless of whether they're designed to be temporary or not. A couple of bad assumptions underlie this approach: the belief that outcomes for any individual worker don't matter, and the belief that there is an infinite supply of workers to fill roles that physically or mentally broken individuals abandon. The former notion can be difficult to challenge if leaders are not possessed of some natural level of empathy, but the latter notion fortunately has been blown to smithereens by pandemic labor shortages. Amazon, for instance, famously worries that they will run out of workers in the United States to staff their ever-larger warehouses.

- *Temporary work turned permanent.* Back to our theme of workplace "kludges," a good deal of unsustainable work was designed with the best of intentions: it wasn't supposed to be sustainable at all! From the hiring of contingent labor to folks stepping into blended roles to replace a coworker who departed unexpectedly, organizations apply any number of work Band-Aids that remain in place years, if not decades later.

  Temporary-turned-permanent solutions don't have to be terrible—sometimes, a working team shapes a temporary solution into an admirable long-term fix. But more often than not, the exigencies of the moment the work is framed in crowds out what's necessary for the work to be done over months or years—anything from "permalancers" needing to receive benefits to actual metrics for success not being set to career paths from the role not being established.

People-Centered Decisions Rebalance the Scales and Restore Your Workplace Equilibrium

Perhaps we need to move the balancing act back from grand initiatives and into a humbler, more prosaic place: the decision. How many times have we looked at a corporate decision and thought, "My God, did they think about [some terrible employee or business impact]?" Did they realize that implementing that new system meant salespeople had less time to spend with customers? Did they realize that promoting Brian would cause five other people who were not Brian to quit? Did they realize that if they didn't give Milton his red stapler, he was in fact going to burn down the building? The answer is, usually they didn't. In the second decade of the twenty-first century, organizations remain remarkably lousy at making decisions, particularly at taking anything other than shareholder/owner value into consideration in those decisions.

Shareholder/owner value is a seductive heuristic for one simple reason: it *seems* quantifiable. Generate enough spreadsheets, and it looks like you can trace any decision's financial impact all the way to the folks holding the company wallet. We then throw up our hands in despair and confusion when over and over again, the Rube Goldberg machine inside the organization breaks. The marble doesn't drop quite right, the mouse refuses to eat the cheese, the weights don't shift, and motion just. . .stops. What happened? People happened! All of those calculations about value generation were precise, but not accurate. The arrow burrows into the target with exactly directed force, but far from the bullseye. People threw it off. Nowhere is this more visible than in the digital transformation space, where an estimated $900 billion a year is wasted on failed technological projects because they didn't work for the people around them.[12]

Part of the issue is that folks making "top-down" decisions about the future of the organization and folks making "bottom-up" decisions about the future of the employee are often either positioned in opposition to each other (finance versus HR! Guess who usually wins that one?) or not really talking to each other at all (when was the last time the Employee Experience group sat down with their peers in Strategic Workforce Planning? Ever?). But on a deeper level, the very notion of "top down" and "bottom up" is a flawed one—as long as we see value awarded to employees as an indulgent subtraction from corporate power or value delivered to shareholders, the modern organization is going to teeter precipitously on the precipice of disaster. We're already seeing this balancing act go awry as labor shortages threaten everything from global supply chains to the basic provision of healthcare. See Figure 4.5.

Better People-Centered Decisions at the Organizational Level: Five Strategies

Utilizing the human-centered decision framework in this chapter isn't complicated—but it isn't always easy, either. Here are five strategies you can use at organizational level to make better people-centered decisions.

- **Strategy 31: Understand when you're making a decision that affects your human workers, know who owns that decision, and identify who's truly affected**. The first six words of this sentence—"understand when you're making a decision"—already present problems for many organizations. Decision-making is often siloed, unconscious, closely held/secretive, or widely diffused. Audits of decision rights may seem to be a dull exercise, but they

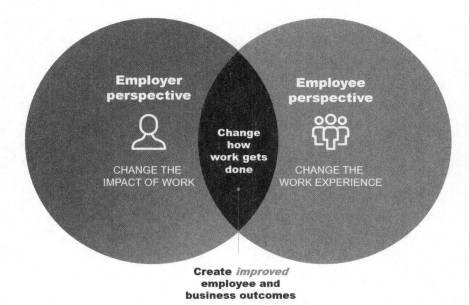

Figure 4.5   How Mercer views workforce transformation

can be illuminating in helping ferret out where decisions are being
made versus where they should be made. Once you've identified
where decisions are happening, and gotten the right owners
involved, leadership will then want to implement programmatic
ways of looking at what humans are affected, how they're affected,
and whether anyone is unintentionally affected. This is not,
incidentally, always an exercise in bad unintended consequences—
Jonathan Feldman, the CIO of Wake County, the county seat of
Raleigh, NC notes, inclusive decisions often have positive impacts
on populations beyond their immediate target. He cites cut curbs
as an example: when curbs are cut down to accommodate people
using wheelchairs, it's also helpful to people with strollers, workers
pushing dolleys, etc. Identifying additional groups impacted by
your decision can actually help pinpoint greater value creation.

- **Strategy 32: Look at the key roles in your organization, and
remove any unneeded qualifications or aspects of work that**

are limiting the talent pool of who can do that work. One great way to get started is with a few pieces of "low-hanging fruit": Are you requiring college degrees for positions where employees don't really need one? Have you eliminated performative work wherever possible, or are many roles biased on that basis toward extroverts? Increased flexibility, organizations are discovering, has the potential to dramatically broaden talent pools for roles. The fewer time-and-place requirements for a role, the more, and the more varied, people available to do it.

- **Strategy 33: Smash your technology silo.** Many decisions that negatively impact human workers have to do with technology. It's tempting to make growling sounds in the direction of the monolithic IT department, but this is an unfair impulse: these folks are often just as nonplussed by their group's scale, complexity, and homogeneity as the business units that have to partner with them are. Help has to come from the top—putting sound, human-centered muscle behind every IT decision. In Chapter 5 we'll go into more detail about how to do so, but one key starting place is to eliminate or reduce structural factors that unintentionally strengthen the IT silo. Simplifying IT organizational structure, creating natural points of intersection with the business, and involving decision-makers from the business early in IT cycles can all reduce frustration down the road.

- **Strategy 34: Make humanism an acceptable part of corporate discourse.** As organizations have grown larger, more complex, and more technology-driven, it has become easier and easier for leaders to speak in rather inhuman terms. We barely even notice anymore that this happens: think of euphemisms like "right-sizing" for layoffs. This seemingly strange way of speaking often has its roots in the need to not spook public markets; you wouldn't want a CEO screaming, "Our results are terrible! As a result we are laying people off! Lots of people!" The problem is, once you start speaking about people in a non-"peoplish" way, your brain subtly dehumanizes them a bit. Do a thought experiment: How does the word "right-sizing" make you feel versus "layoffs"? The second word has an emotional impact, doesn't it? Reintroducing words with emotional connotation into corporate conversation may seem awkward at first—like writing with a pen in your nondominant hand—but this awkwardness is actually some repressed humanity reasserting itself. Do this consistently across a large enough group of executives, and more human-centered decisions should result.

- **Strategy 35: Examine roles designed for obsolescence—do they have features you'd consider unacceptable in longer-term roles?** No organization would construct temporary work—be it a 2-year analyst or an 8-week Christmas elf—exactly like more permanent work. This doesn't mean that temporary work should operate without guardrails. Temporary work is particularly prone to intensification, on the assumption that these workers can do more because they're doing it for a shorter period of time. Examining temporary work for excess intensification can both accelerate productivity and increase retention—if workers are operating in conditions of burnout, they may be doing less and quitting more often, which even in the context of "not-forever" jobs can be a drain on your organization.

Better People-Centered Decisions at the Team Level: Five Strategies

It's funny: sometimes we're better at thinking like humans at organizational level than team level. We can all agree that things need to operate a certain way, but when it comes to our own team, we're prone to going on autopilot and being a bit insensitive. Here are five strategies to make more human-centered decisions on team level:

- **Strategy 36: Model humanism—including self-care.** Want work to operate in a more human way? As a leader, show up at work as a human. It's simple advice that can be tough to implement in many corporate cultures. I've certainly worked in offices where they made you feel like you had to be slick, perfect, and hard-shelled. . .*or else.* But even in those environments, I have found that demonstrating vulnerability (communicating about feeling lost, for instance) and being honest about "human stuff" (like needing to leave early to pick up my daughter) have created a better way of operating in my immediate teams.

- **Strategy #: Identify and obliterate "kludges" and temporary solutions that have accidentally become permanent.** In real life, kludges can be easy to spot: you can probably find one by taking a look around your house. (For us, it's a Tupperware sitting behind one sink, catching the occasional drip from a piece of plumbing that really needs to be replaced!) At work, though, they often blend seamlessly into the flow of how things get done day to day, which is why they persist for so long. A quick audit of temporary-turned-permanent solutions should focus on three categories: (1) temporary roles turned permanent (look for years of 1099s. . .); (2) temporary processes turned permanent (look for processes that are mysteriously not documented anywhere); and (3) temporary tech turned permanent (get a good list of what people are actually using—then match it up to what IT and business leadership *think* they're using). The discrepancies you'll identify can be shocking, particularly on the workforce front. My colleague, Karen Piercy, a 30-year specialist in the transformation of HR departments, often sees organizations filling *30% to 40% of roles* via temporary labor on a permanent basis, unintentionally. That's an outstanding percentage of your workforce to have hired by accident! We'll explore this topic in greater depth in Chapter 6.

- **Strategy 38: Plan like a pessimist.** Any time you implement a new technology or process, have a plan B, a plan C, and a plan D. Then measure whether workers' lives got easier or harder. In the military, this process is commonplace—leaders will look at all the ways an action can fail before the action is taken and plan accordingly. Seems like a no-brainer, right? But in the context of multi-million-dollar technology implementations, where executives often feel like their jobs are on the line, discussions of failure can be taboo. Despite the allegedly rational nature of these processes, our behavior can be downright superstitious—it's as if we fear drawing "the evil eye" by mentioning that technology doesn't always work perfectly. Wake County CIO Jonathan Feldman cites leaders' need for "self-preservation" as the killer factor here—when technology implementations operate as "get-rich-quick" schemes to solve a host of problems that no tech on its own could solve for, the deck is stacked against doing the right thing. A moment of leadership bravery is what's called for: sitting down with your stakeholders to talk about the worst-case scenario effectively ensures it won't happen.

- **Strategy 39: Figure out your hidden talent acquisition hurdles to maximize inclusion.** In Chapter 3, we talked about stopping your team from hiring the same folks ("replicants") over and over. Part of doing so is figuring out the hidden blockers—what do you assume is needed for roles on your team that might not be needed? Do you have implicit assumptions about everything from skills to geography to educational background? Might you be eliminating scores of qualified candidates for no reason at all, or for reasons that have more to do with personal preference? A quick audit could completely blow up your talent pipeline, in a good way.

- **Strategy 40: Have a few mental models for what "overwhelmed" looks like—and a playbook of strategies to address issues *before* individuals are in full burnout.** When speaking to audiences during the Great Resignation, the question I get most often is a poignant one: How, especially in virtual settings, can I tell if someone is starting to burn out or face mental challenges at work? It would be great to be able to say, "watch for these five things," but the reality is far more complicated. How mental health struggles show up varies wildly across individuals from different backgrounds— cultural conditioning as well as individual personality differences make people more and less likely to be vocal or display certain emotions. If workers feel at all professionally vulnerable, they're also more likely to conceal their symptoms—to their detriment and yours. It's critical, then, for leaders to understand a few different models of how diminished mental health may show up, including both "quiet" and "loud" symptoms. Similarly, when it comes to intervening, one size doesn't fit all either; be prepared to deploy anything from employee assistance programs to active listening to reworked workloads, or a combination of all of the above.

Human-centric decision-making will feel very natural sometimes and quite challenging at others. If you think about it, there's something interesting about the fact that we even have to modify "decision-making" with the adjective "human-centric"—we've insufficiently accounted for human beings in how we make decisions to date.

One outgrowth of this strange deprioritization of humans is that we've put technology on pedestal in unproductive ways—squandering the truly immense potential of that technology. In Chapter 5, we'll look at how that disconnect is playing out across the human experience of work—and what we can do to get humans and technology working better together.

5 Tech Dreams, Tech Nightmares

Couples Counseling for Humans and Technology

"Computers are useless. They can only give you answers."

—Pablo Picasso

If we had to assign a Facebook relationship status to humans and technology at work, it would definitely be "it's complicated." While technology has unquestionably revolutionized what's possible across roles from front line to C-suite on a day-to-day basis, it also frustrates us and even exhausts us.

While an entire chapter about all the ways that technology drives us crazy at work would be incredibly cathartic to write, and likely pretty amusing for you to read, just kvetching wouldn't actually be helpful. So while we'll start with a quick account of where work technology often does more harm than good, we'll then move on to some of the surprising reasons *why* our experience of technology at work is so crummy—and then finally we'll explore how to make your organization's experience of and value derived from technology as great as possible. Because the promise of technology at work truly is bright—if we can harness it to a human way of working. Technology itself gets a bad rap; fix using our approach, and the systems we rely on can go from dystopian to utopian in a flash.

Tech at Work: The Problem

Problematic technology at work haunts our collective dreams. Virtually any movie set in the workplace features some moment where technology goes haywire. If you're GenX, like me, *Office Space's* repeated error message "PC Load Letter"—provoking the main characters to destroy a printer with a baseball bat—perfectly captures a certain kind of low-level tech failure that quietly makes your job impossible. Slightly older movie fans might recall the printer in *9 to 5* spitting out a rainbow-colored array of paper at demonic speed, or think of Stanley Kubrick's iconic *2001*, where the whole plot revolves around a computer that decides it knows better than the humans around it, with disastrous consequences (Figure 5.1).

Figure 5.1   *2001: A Space Odyssey* **poster**

Source: Allstar Picture Library Limited / Alamy Images.

Weirdly, the biggest, most prominent technology failures *aren't* the problem. While massive systems crashes make the headlines, organizations generally have some level of capability to address these issues. When a catastrophic event happens, they mobilize large groups of personnel to respond—often using predetermined protocols that provide some sort of a "script" for how to handle the problem. These responses may not always go well—think of how many companies have been temporarily hobbled by data breaches, for instance, in recent years—but for the highest profile issues, companies generally equip themselves with resources and a template to try and solve.

It's not the big catastrophes dragging us down. It's the many, many little moments where technology just doesn't quite work right. These moments can be hilarious—think of the poor lawyer accidentally wearing a "kitten" filter on a Zoom call with a judge, protesting that he was not, in fact, a cat![1] There are also ominous moments where, like the evil computer Hal in *2001*, technology jumps in and shapes our behavior in undesirable ways. In New York City today, pedestrians are forced to dodge an ever-burgeoning array of delivery drivers on electric bikes—barreling along at excessive speed across roads and sidewalks alike because an app's algorithm told them it "should" take a certain amount of time to make a particular delivery.

The cat-faced lawyer is funny; nearly getting killed by a bike messenger toting rotisserie chicken is not. In between those two extremes lies a world of low-grade but pervasive frustration. A study conducted by tech firm Citrix in 2021 perfectly captures this dynamic: the researchers found that 71% of the employees they surveyed believed collaboration and communication technology had made their work more complex.[2] The study noted that 33% of workers dealt with 10–20 *different* communication or collaboration technologies in a day, which is tiring even if they all work perfectly. Of those surveyed, 18% had considered quitting due to bad technology experiences,[3] which is not terribly surprising given the research we examined previously, in which nearly half of time using technology at work was believed to be wasted.[4]

The rapid pace of technological change was supposed to solve technological frustrations for many, but in many cases, the opposite occurs: new technology drives us even crazier. A Gartner study found that 60% of workers had gotten frustrated with new software in the last 2 years, and that 56% of workers surveyed actually wanted the old technology back, a dispiriting message to organizations who spend billions on technological upgrades.[5]

Where is tech going wrong? We can separate issues into four broad categories: why it's being implemented, how it's being built, how tech and humans work together, and the world it's being built in.

We Have Seen the Enemy and It Is Us: Technology as a Leadership Band-Aid

When we start to unpack our frustrations with technology, let's first point the lens at the folks responsible: people. Wake County CIO Jonathan Feldman, North Carolina, explains:

> This notion that technology is the enemy is tempting. . .but it turns out that it's the people that are procuring and implementing the technology that suck.
>
> —Jonathan Feldman, CIO of the city of Asheville, NC.

When we start to unpack the role of leaders in bad tech, we come back to a version of the Work Anxiety Monster. Leaders today are confronted with ever more complex and intractable issues and don't always feel up to the challenge of truly solving seemingly unsolvable problems. As Feldman explains, at its worst technology can be the "snake oil" they reach for:

> You know how people are addicted to get rich quick schemes. I think people want to believe the too good to be true scenario.

When someone brings a project to me, and they say, well we just need to buy this software—I think it's driven by the same kind of simplistic, instant gratification [thinking]. . .tech feels like a shortcut that avoids doing all of the icky stuff. And it's actually a time bomb.

The time bomb language is scary, but apt. When technology is deployed as a Band-Aid instead of sutures, a host of issues result. Often, a system or piece of software is meant to serve as the simple solution to a complex, multifaceted problem, so while it does solve some subpart of the problem, a host of other issues persist, making us frustrated that the technology didn't solve an array of problems that it never could have solved in the first place.

"Systems of record" are particularly prone to this sort of challenge—simply having a place to record all of the information about something doesn't mean you can then make sense of that information. It doesn't mean that people entered all the right information, or entered information consistently. It doesn't mean anyone knows how to conduct the right analytics on that information or that leaders will look at any of the information or analytics or that they can interpret any of those analytics properly. In short—you still have most of the problems you had before implementing the system. . .and it's not the system's fault. It's your organization's. My colleague, Julie Humphries, who leads Mercer's Digital practice, notes that many technology implementations actually fail before they begin by neglecting the process of integrating the technology into the organization's way of working from the beginning, addressing this crucial step far too late:

> The most important element of any technology implementation focuses on adoption strategy in order to ensure the targeted outcome. Rather than positioning change management at the end of an implementation, the key to success is just the opposite— beginning the project with the end user front and center, defining

streamlined business processes that truly elevate overall user experience.

—Julie Humphries

The more advanced the technology—and thus the less understood—the more alluring it can be as a panacea for deep organizational problems no technology could ever solve. I can't tell you how many clients have shared tales of woe about frantic chases for AI and predictive analytic solutions to problems that could have been solved in a simple Excel spreadsheet if someone really understood the underlying business issue enough to frame the question. It's as if leaders are living out Arthur C. Clarke's famous assertion that "any sufficiently advanced technology is indistinguishable from magic" and treating technology as if it can transmute the straw of difficult business problems into the gold of easy solutions. In reality, interpreting many aspects of the business world is a task so complex that even the most advanced technology could barely chip away at the most surface insights. I find that the practitioners who know the *most* about advanced analytics are, across the board, most skeptical about its technology-driven applications. For instance, Haig Nalbantian, a cofounder of Mercer's Workforce Sciences Institute, notes, "I don't think AI can capture the complexities of interactions within systems of HR practice and workforce events that deliver the most profound insights."[6] The more savvy you are, the less appealing technology is as a Band-Aid for every business problem.

But leaders often aren't so savvy. Recent Massachusetts Institute of Technology research showed that only one in four chief executive officers (CEOs) were digitally savvy, and one in eight chief financial officers (CFOs). These statistics are alarming, but perhaps not as alarming as the fact that the same study found that slightly less than half of both CIOs and chief technology officers (CTOs) were digitally savvy.[7] If less than half of the executives *explicitly charged with leading the technology journey* are up to speed on the latest technology, really, what hope is there for the rest of us?

We get reminded of the limitations of our collective tech knowledge every so often when a scandal like Theranos hits— showing the consequences of smiling and nodding and not asking questions—but it is daily reality across many organizations as executives frantically try to save face amidst a ceaseless march of technology. Interestingly, this behavior cuts both ways—both triggering waves of needless technology adoption and sometimes blocking needed adoption too, as clueless executives try to avoid a technological conversation altogether.

The end result of this large-scale cover-up of leaders' missing tech savvy is that workers are inundated with technology that is irrelevant, misguided, or redundant. In a best-case scenario, there's some leader in the equation to stop the madness (Feldman wryly notes, "If you just bring me technology as a shortcut, I look at you like you have just clicked on the 'punch the monkey and get $10,000' button"), but many organizations do not have that person. And technological experience at work suffers mightily as a result.

Eternal Minimum Viable Product: Why the Genius of Iterative Tech Also Makes Us Crazy

Part of the issue with hard-to-use technology at work also lurks behind the scenes. Thanks to development processes like Agile—and the incredible flexibility that Cloud deployment gives us—we are often working on software that's, well, not quite final. That's by design—no one's trying to serve you an underbaked cake, tech-wise— but when we look for the deep roots of tech that always seems to *kind of* work, the actual technical details of software building and deployment really turn out to matter to an employee's experience of using it.

Broadly speaking, technology today gets built in one of two ways: waterfall or Agile (Agile being inclusive of similar processes like DevOps). In waterfall-style development, software is built in a highly linear fashion, starting with requirements development, and released following robust testing.

And Agile? Let's start with the most basic explanation: the Agile Manifesto, written by a group of developers in Snowbird, Utah, in 2001. Unlike the millions of words that seem to have been written about Agile ever since then, the Manifesto itself is just 68 words (one-third the length of the Gettysburg Address!) Here it is in its entirety (Figure 5.2):

> We are uncovering better ways of developing software by doing it and helping others do it.
>
> Through this work we have come to value:
>
> Individuals and interactions over processes and tools
>
> Working software over comprehensive documentation
>
> Customer collaboration over contract negotiation
>
> Responding to change over following a plan
>
> That is, while there is value in the items on the right, we value the items on the left more.
>
> —Agilemanifesto.org, Manifesto for Agile Software Development. Last accessed by July 27, 2022.

In practice, what this means in simplest form is that when we build software in Agile, we develop it to "minimum viable product" level, get it to the testers that matter—the real world—and then iterate from there. For years, the technology world treated Agile as a savior—demolishing the bureaucratic nightmare of building software step by step against elaborately developed requirements. The advent of Cloud deployment for software only boosted what could be accomplished via

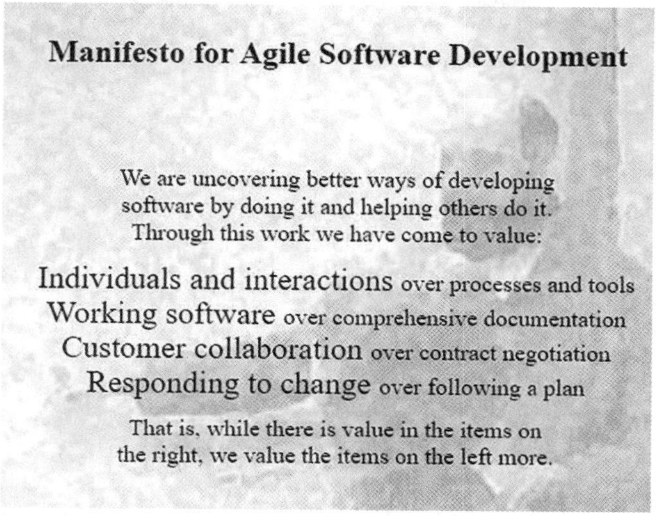

Manifesto for Agile Software Development

We are uncovering better ways of developing
software by doing it and helping others do it.
Through this work we have come to value:

Individuals and interactions over processes and tools
Working software over comprehensive documentation
Customer collaboration over contract negotiation
Responding to change over following a plan

That is, while there is value in the items on
the right, we value the items on the left more.

Figure 5.2   Agile Manifesto

Source: Agilemanifesto.org, Manifesto for Agile Software Development. Last accessed by July 27, 2022.

Agile processes—the whole debate about "when to ship" software gets a lot less fraught when you're not physically "shipping" anything!

To understand the critique of Agile, think of the main character, Leonard, in the film *Memento*. Robbed of his memory beyond 15 minute increments, all he can do is assess each situation he finds himself in, and try to get to the best possible result. He's in motion throughout the film—fighting bad guys and solving puzzles.

The problem—with apologies for spoilers for a 20-year-old movie—is that while Leonard undertakes a series of actions that are each rational in the moment, we learn at the end that it all adds up to him living a lie. He's perfectly Agile, but the Waterfall aspects of his world are the true governing forces.

For many folks, unfortunately, this is Agile—dashing memorylessly through a world where deeper forces pull all the strings. It can be a challenging formula for software that's pressed to solve complex problems.

There are, also, some very wrong times for Agile, when you can't afford to test and learn with real people. As Wake County CIO Jonathan Feldman explains,

> Agile is not an everything type of practice. No one builds a skyscraper with Agile. When we deployed a $6m radio infrastructure project for public safety—with functionality to tell us automatically when a police officer has been shot—no, that's gonna be waterfall. Because if we get it wrong, people could die!
>
> —Jonathan Feldman, CIO of the city of Asheville, NC.

Not every use case is as stark as "officer down" functionality, which leaves most of us working with software that is somewhere between Agile and Waterfall world—between minimum viable product and a polished final result. The assumption being that new versions can get deployed as improvements are made. IT departments are walking a fine line—trying to get new functionality to employees to do more as soon as possible while not creating a fundamentally clunky user experience.

While we may joke that technology is "Jetsons at home, Flintstones at work," the reality is that we do the same dance through a world of semi-finished tech in our personal lives. Think of the apps you use on your phone—how many look the same as they did a year ago? Or do the same things? Not many—we're used to a world of constant updates, not all of them felicitous. What's thrown us off is consumer-grade *hardware*. The elegance of contemporary smartphones, in particular, has given us the illusion of technological perfection—even as many of the apps on those phones may just barely work half the time.

So here we sit—in a world where, for better *and* for worse, we can get software out relatively quickly—reaping both the rewards and the consequences. Would it be better to only ever use perfectly refined software, likely months or years after it has ceased to be relevant? Absolutely not. But do we need a better way of thinking about working on some version of minimum viable product all the time? For sure we do.

Tech and Humans: The *I Love Lucy* Problem

Are you familiar with the *I Love Lucy* episode "Job Switching" (Figure 5.3)? You may not know the title, but you've likely seen the scene it's famous for—where Lucy and Ethel melt down in a chocolate factory, no pun intended. Having switched places with their husbands due to a fight over spending (and believe me, there's a whole other book to be written about that piece alone), they're berated by their supervisor for not packing chocolates fast enough. As an unforgiving assembly line careens chocolate after chocolate at our hapless heroines, their panic deepens. Faced with the prospect of an unhappy supervisor, they frantically hide unwrapped chocolates by stuffing them into their mouths and clothes—pleasing their boss, but prompting her to speed up the assembly line even further!

And that's the *I Love Lucy* problem in a nutshell. It's both possible, and tempting, to create technology that works faster than humans can. If we believe humans are slow and lazy, why not give

Figure 5.3   *I Love Lucy,* "Job Switching"
Source: CBS Photo Archive / Getty Images.

them a little tech boost? We can set the pace in an automated fashion, and the people involved will speed up accordingly, right?

Maybe. Maybe not. A 2019 report on technological change in the warehouse environment from the University of Berkeley Labor Center and Working Partnerships USA[8] highlights the work intensification that results when warehouses utilize more automation—both physical (robotics) and behind the scenes (data-driven management by algorithm). They describe a world in which technology has made work far more stressful and anxious:

> This data has the potential to increase pressure to work quickly. . .Digital Taylorism is well under way in some parts of the warehousing industry. . . .Careful tracking of productivity has led to termination when employees are not reaching the target rate, and workers report feeling anxiety about the possibility of being terminated.

The Berkeley report notes a critical problem with pacesetting tech: similar to the old adage about teaching the cat to dance both driving you crazy and annoying the cat, technology that sets a pace faster than humans can work can both drive workers to mental and physical ruin *and* destroy far more productivity than it creates:

> Rising productivity requirements also raise questions about the limits of the human body, and there are concerns that such close scrutiny over workers' movements could have detrimental psychological impacts. The assumption that streamlining processes leads in a linear fashion to greater efficiencies, and thus cost reductions, may be fundamentally flawed. Gains could be counteracted by new health and safety hazards, as well as increased employee turnover due to overwork and burnout. The toll on workers is both physical and psychological, as increased performance metrics may push workers to exhaustion while

heightening anxieties over the threat of being dismissed for missing performance targets. The unintended consequences of work intensification, therefore, could aggravate the challenge of recruiting and retaining workers, especially in tight labor markets.

There's a lot of bad news in that one paragraph. Physical and mental harm to workers. Inefficient processes and cost overruns. Talent shortages. All prescient observations for 2019—in the early 2020s, this is exactly what we're seeing day to day, amidst headlines trumpeting supply chain breakdowns and business-threatening worker scarcity.

It's time to quiet the Work Anxiety Monster's voice telling us it's all too slow and get technology working at human speed.

Cyber Issues

Finally, when it comes to bad tech at work, there are actual villains. An ever-escalating number of cyberattacks have created a constant atmosphere of threat and sent organizations scrambling to fend off would-be catastrophes. During the pandemic period, increased reliance on digital tools doubled down on this phenomenon. Ramy Houssaini, chief cyber and technology risk officer and group privacy officer of BNP Paribas, explains: "We have dealt over the past couple of years with a cyber pandemic that is still ongoing and unfortunately for which there are no vaccines. This whole new digital experience is happening in an increasingly hostile environment."

Why does this matter to the user experience of workers? Sadly, most measures to make digital interaction safer also slow it down. Imagine a bike with training wheels: it's harder to fall over, but you can't exactly zoom down the street. You can have safety or effortless speed—but not both. And in this "cyber pandemic," organizations *have* to choose safety. Which means that their employees fight their way through an impenetrable jungle of endless updates, two-factor authentication, elaborate password changes, and other measures that sometimes add hours to the workday. If you've ever changed your password to something like "PsswdsAreEvl@321," you know what I'm talking about.

Government plays a role in solving the cyber crisis, but as we work ever more globally, a patchwork of different government regulations around security and privacy slow the everyday experience of tech down even further. Houssaini explains:

> We're all suffering from this regulatory fragmentation. If you operate as a global actor, you are subject to very different expectations and trying to come up with a baseline that would allow you to operate globally with that agility while meeting the local requirements can be extremely difficult.

On the cyber front, at least, there is some hope on the horizon. Houssaini describes a future in which ambient, native controls minimize friction, and better "digital citizens" with greater cyber awareness need less protection from themselves.

Until then, we'll have to get comfortable moving at training-wheels speed sometimes, even when it feels like the business is in the Tour De France.

What to Do: Organization Level

The following strategies for realigning technology to business priorities and user experience aren't offered lightly. If 70% to 84% of digital transformations actually fail, it's certainly not because it's easy to get humans and technology into "couples counseling" together![9] Overcoming some of the chafing points discussed in this chapter requires a healthy dose of leader and organizational humility and a willingness to engage with tangled layers of complexity in the current environment.

- **Strategy 41: Obsess over tech governance.** Compared to other technology topics, governance is not a terribly exciting theme. The phrase "tech governance" may even evoke negative associations for both IT and the functions and business areas IT partners with—calling to mind endless hours of meetings with dozens of stakeholders. That said, any organization that truly gets its arms around who makes what technology decision, as well as when and why those decisions get made, will see the storm clouds of confusion part and a new era of sanity come shining through. Reasonable goals include reducing the number of people who request and approve added technologies, ensuring that both business and IT leaders are accountable for both business outcomes and user experience, and putting into place some sort of regular audit mechanism to ensure historical technology decisions continue to make sense in a rapidly-shifting environment.

- **Strategy 42: Make sure you're choosing tech for the right reasons—and then make sure you're re-choosing it.** With sensible governance in place around making decisions, it's then time to take a hard look at how those decisions are made. Wake County CIO Jonathan Feldman has a list of standard questions he asks during conversations about introducing a new technology: *"What are you trying to solve? Who are you trying to solve for? Do you want to solve it for others? Are you sure that's who you want to solve it for?"* Institutionalizing simple analysis around business and stakeholder impact sounds absurdly basic, but in many organizations, even sophisticated ones, these foundational conversations are skipped or go haywire. Moreover, technology implemented on an "emergency" or "temporary" basis has, as Feldman notes, a nasty habit of sticking around; savvy leaders routinely ask the question of whether a "quick fix" has outlived its usefulness, or at least requires some shoring up.

- **Strategy 43: Marie Kondo your tech stack—using an employee's-eye view.** Think of your organization's tech stack like your kitchen. Over time, you may end up with a lot of different appliances: a mixer, a blender, a food processor, a toaster oven, a waffle maker, a mini-cupcake maker, a rice cooker, that weird thing that makes "ice cream" from frozen bananas. One day you turn around and a small army of electronics are staring back at you from your countertop. It's easy to end up with a lot of technology, in a kitchen or a company. In your kitchen, you'd take a step back and say, "Is anyone really eating waffles? Could we make mini-cupcakes in the toaster oven instead? Is frozen banana ice cream actually disgusting?" At an organizational level, the same process is very much worth doing, and you'll want to use an employee lens, asking simple questions and then acting on the answers. Good questions would include, "What technology is actually being used, to what extent, and by whom?" "What technology reliably drives workers crazy?" "What technologies might be redundant with each other?" The goal isn't full, classic optimization from a cost or systems perspective: you may decide, for instance, that it's okay if two different groups use different technologies for the same thing if their needs are different enough and the systems don't need to "talk" to each other. A better goal would be "least possible number of technologies to get the work done with a basically pleasant user experience."

- **Strategy 44: Have an honest conversation about cybersecurity—and what it's going to *feel* like.** Efforts to educate employees about cybersecurity traditionally focus, rightly, on avoiding incidents such as phishing attacks. Rarely do organizations step back and provide broader context around the environment they're operating in and how cyber protection is actually brought to operational reality. It's the rare employee who can connect security needs with the constant updates and associated reboots that seemingly threaten to overturn productivity altogether. Organizations would do well to foster an honest and candid dialogue about why, in the interests of business continuity, user experience might feel a bit choppier than we'd like at times.

- **Strategy 45: Make sure tech is working at the speed of humans and not vice versa.** Technology can play a wonderful role in helping us do things better, and where appropriate, faster. Do I get more steps a day because I track them on my Fitbit? Can I run faster on a treadmill than on the New York City streets? Yes and yes. But does my Fitbit sometimes give me unreasonable cues, like telling me I need to get up and move around while on a flight with the "Fasten Seatbelts" sign on? Yup. Would I fall flat on my face on a treadmill turned up to 5-minute miles, and is it often preferable to run a bit slower but get exposed to the early morning sunlight? Yes to both of those as well. At work, we need to be conscious of whether technology has the treadmill going too fast: too many boxes to pack in an hour, too many Outlook meetings in a day. Collecting real-time employee feedback on this front can be helpful and can avoid being alerted to the problem by lagging indicators of tech-harried employees (everything from workers' compensation claims to mass resignations). We also need to watch for technological miscues, like the Fitbit telling me to stand up as my plane is going through turbulence. Often these miscues are subtle, but powerful—such as an organization trying to fight employee burnout whose automated training reminders went out on Sundays.

What to Do: Team Level

Trying to grapple with worker experience of technology at the team level can feel exhausting and disheartening. Even in organizations with thoughtful tech governance, individual leaders may struggle to understand what impact they can have on broader decisions about technology used by their team. That's why, in the following strategies, you'll see an emphasis at the team level on the role of communication. Remember the old ads that admonished parents, "Talk to your kids about drugs, or someone else will"? Here the thought would be, "Talk to your team about technology, or they'll imagine the worst themselves." Here are some communications-laden strategies to help your team better harness technological resources for good, not frustration:

- **Strategy 46: Agree on your comms tech.** Across many organizations, during the COVID-19 period we realized something fundamental: we need to talk about how we talk to each other. Once we couldn't connect across the water cooler, organizations reached for a dizzying array of tools to create human connections—everything from sophisticated videoconferencing to basic text message apps. As with many technological questions, there's no "right" answer here; it is, however, critical to get agreement at team level about the small array of communications technologies *that work for the team*. Much as we say in photography that the best camera is the one you have with you, the best communications technology is the one your team will collectively, consistently use. You may need a handful of technologies, but curate the ecosystem down as much as possible—switching from tech to tech drives worker exhaustion.

- **Strategy 47: Take tech gripes seriously—and *ask* about your team's experience of tech.** Are you, yourself, a "boiled frog" on the technology front? Has the temperature of technological annoyance been raised so slowly over many years that you no longer feel that the climate is unliveable? Time to "unboil" yourself. Engage your team in a dialogue about what technology is and is not working for them, listen acutely, and take action on the most prevalent complaints, even if they sound silly. Over time, banal issues like documents taking a long time to open snowball into deep and persistent frustration and productivity loss. Our data show this effect—positive responses to a typical engagement survey item, "I have the appropriate technical resources, software, and IT support needed to do my job" correlate strongly to a survey item that measures retention, "I would choose to stay with my company even if offered the same pay and benefits elsewhere." Tech that works matters.

- **Strategy 48: Set realistic expectations around software and hardware.** Not all software is created equal, nor is all hardware. Setting realistic expectations for what the experience of technology will be can help tamp down frustrations. Talk to your team about what technology operates in a more rough-and-ready fashion, and where they can expect a smoother user experience. Acknowledge that both hardware and software are designed for particular use cases, and that they may begin to act funny under different conditions. Perhaps the most visible example of this phenomenon has come during the pandemic period, as laptops have been challenged to undertake the workload of desktop machines. . .and have experienced everything from slow processors to loud fans to slowly exploding batteries. If you know your laptop is being stretched, the battery fighting its way out of the case may get a bit less alarming!

- **Strategy 49: Volunteer your team aggressively as beta testers.** How many times has technology shown up on your team's doorstep and after a few days of using it, everyone huffs and puffs about, "Did no one try any of this out?" There's a remedy—in many organizations, teams can put their hands up to be early users of technology, providing vital feedback to help calibrate functionality and user experience *before* the official roll-out. Leaders often shy away from participating in these exercises because they seem like extra work for the team, but in reality, the opportunity to provide feedback both concretely helps the team's eventual experience and generates a sense of genuine empowerment. If you're a beta tester, technology isn't just something that happens to you.

- **Strategy 50: Make friends with your CIO.** The IT world can be intimidating: lots of jargon, lots of complexity, scary budgets. But getting over the intimidation factor is truly, unquestionably worth it. Befriend your CIO, and you'll quickly realize that in many cases the organization's seemingly least accessible function is in fact the one populated by the folks most eager to partner. Working in the digital transformation space, I've had the pleasure of spending years in and around the CIO community and experienced an incredible spirit of collaboration, warmth, and inclusion. Today's technologists, counter to stereotypes, are a diverse array of smart business thinkers with a sincere interest in building better empathy into tech. Engaging your CIO and their team is time well spent.

As frustrating as today's era of iffy technology can be, implementing the strategies in this chapter can help carry teams and organizations to an exciting place. Thinking about the Arthur C. Clarke quote from earlier in the chapter, when technology truly *is* so advanced as to be indistinguishable from magic, the experience and the impact of our work are truly transformed.

Now that we've talked about technology, let's turn the lens back to people—and how, counterintuitively, sometimes the best thing we can do is ignore them as individuals. In the next chapter, we'll look at the power of taking pressure off each employee and turning the heat up on getting the people *system* right.

6 The Intentional Workforce

Combatting the Great Resignation by Managing Working Populations More Thoughtfully

"If there were somewhere else that valued loyalty more highly, I'm going wherever they value loyalty the most."

—Dwight Schrute, *The Office*

The night of October 8, 1871, legend has it, Mrs. O'Leary's cow kicked over a lantern, starting the Great Chicago Fire. A good portion of the city burned down as a result, and 300 lives were lost. What's remarkable about the Great Chicago Fire, though, is not that it set a new benchmark for bovine destruction, but that ultimately it occasioned a truly thoughtful rebuilding of the city, including the architectural marvels of the Chicago School.

Coming, slowly, out of the most active period of the COVID-19 pandemic, and while the associated labor crisis rages on, organizations have a similar opportunity: to turn a painful disaster into an opportunity to, to steal President Biden's phrase, "build back better." This chapter focuses on a few areas of opportunity to think about working populations more thoughtfully, creating an intentional workforce.

First, we'll examine some deep structural issues in working populations that Mercer research has uncovered, delving into the causes of the Great Resignation by looking at all the ways "your mileage may vary" at work, depending on demographics. After all, if we can truly wrap our arms around how experiences vary, we can better attract and retain the talent we value deeply, and run more efficiently and effectively. We'll then examine another area where unintentional choices have shaped workforces for the worse: the ever-deepening challenges of contingent workforces, where organizations quietly suffer all kinds of economic challenges. Finally, we'll look at an under-explored lever for re-gearing the workforce: issues in performance management and how we might reshape this moribund area to properly retain and reward the workforces we *want*.

In the Wake of the Pandemic, Further Evidence That Different Groups Truly Experience Work Differently

As the conversation around equity in the workforce continues to evolve, and organizations have continued to experience labor shortages, Mercer set out to understand, at a fundamental level, how different populations' experiences of both work and how they're rewarded might vary. To better understand how organizations could combat an ever-more expensive talent crisis, we studied 2,000 workers at organizations with 500+ employees—half salaried, half hourly.[1]

Even as an organization that studies these topics regularly—and conducted a wide array of research particularly during the pandemic period—we were surprised by what we found.

The first shocker: even during the height of the "Great Resignation," the portion of workers considering leaving their jobs,

28%, was identical to historical norms. This one had us scratching our heads. But then we dug deeper. It turned out that certain population groups *were* far more likely to think about leaving their jobs—and there was an eerie logic to which groups felt that way. We determined that three categories of employees were deeply dissatisfied and potentially looking for other jobs:

- *Groups who've experienced demographically based discrimination:* In our survey results, Black employees were 10 percentage points more likely than White employees to be considering leaving their roles (35% versus 25%) with Asian-American employees 15 percentage points more likely to leave (40% versus 25%). What's going on here?

  Ballard Spahr's chief diversity, equity, and inclusion officer, Virginia Essandoh, explains how long-term, pervasive gaps in appreciation for performance can, quite logically, make diverse talent less "sticky" to organizations:

  For diverse talent, the competitor next door calling and whispering in your ear about how much they want you and how much value you would bring to their team, and they are offering a significant salary increase—that might appeal to you in a way that it might not appeal to your white colleague. Your white colleague might say, but you're not giving me anything more than I'd get here. It is a privilege of confidence, comfort, and belonging when it is demonstrated that you are valued and that you are on track for continued success. But if diverse talent is not intentionally valued in the workplace, hearing it from a competitor might just be the tipping point to make you leave.

  Essandoh's description is powerful and heartbreaking. Most employers wouldn't consciously devalue entire swaths of the population, and yet our data show that that message has been delivered anyway—at scale. An array of other studies show the same effect—Black employees manifest higher turnover rates across the board.[2] For organizations, this means that both the dollars spent on attracting and hiring this group, and their contributions once at work, are being needlessly wasted. It's both an ethical and an economic burn.

- *Groups who are more loosely tied to their employers by virtue of lifecycle or role:* As a society, we put a lot on the shoulders of two groups in the workforce to whom we do not pay a lot of money: hourly workers and entry-level workers. We take for granted an endless stream of folks doing everything from packing boxes in warehouses to staffing fast-food restaurants to entering reams of data and filing forests' worth of documents. Were these groups to vanish, we'd be in serious trouble—as recent supply chain shortages have graphically demonstrated. And they're unhappy— far more so than their salaried or longer-tenured peers. In our study, 42% of entry-level personnel were considering leaving their jobs—versus only 24% of managers and 15% of executives. Similarly, 37% of hourly workers and 37% of low-wage workers (earning less than $60,000/year) were prone to make a jump, while only 23% of those making more than $60,000 were considering leaving their roles.

- *Groups in industries with long-standing structural issues that flared during the pandemic:* It's not a surprising statement to say that healthcare or retail jobs are tough. These roles often involve hours on your feet and significant emotional labor. During the pandemic, the challenges in these roles were multiplied a thousand-fold as hospitals grew overloaded, customers grew contentious, and workers in both industries struggled with day-to-day health and safety concerns without easy solutions. Accordingly, we saw in our data a chasm between the inclination of these groups to look for a new job—37% in retail and 34% in healthcare—and that of their peers in industries that didn't feature long-running structural issues—22% in high tech and 21% in professional services. See Figure 6.1.

Unmet Needs: Chasing the "Why" of Attrition

More surprising than the disparities by population in desire to leave one's job was what we found in terms of differences in unmet needs between these populations—the things pushing workers out the door.

Let's start with the baseline—what were the top unmet needs across the overall working population surveyed? Across *all* workers, the top four unmet needs were, respectively, physical health, work–life balance, mental/emotional health, and personal fulfillment/purpose. These are not surprising findings for the COVID-19 period, where wellness and purpose truly rose to the top of workers' agendas.

What's striking is how different unmet needs vary across populations. Remember the low-wage workers who were far more likely to leave their roles? They cited covering monthly expenses as their number 1 unmet need—and being able to retire as number 4.

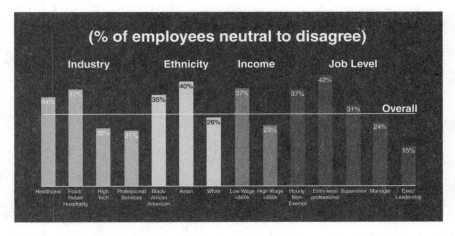

Figure 6.1   From Mercer Data, who's thinking about quitting?

As a group, they rated clearing personal debt as a much more deeply felt unmet need than the overall population did. For this group, where wages have long lagged inflation, financial concerns clearly crowd out other worries.

Black workers also cited dramatically different unmet needs than workers of other ethnicities. Heartbreakingly, this group cited personal safety as their primary unmet need at work, which speaks deeply to a different experience not just at work, but in life. Black workers were also markedly more likely than the overall population to cite mental health and covering monthly expenses as unmet needs, speaking to this group not feeling the same basic support net as others.

Finally, workers' unmet needs also varied among age groups in telling ways. Mental health was the number 1 unmet need for the youngest age groups, who were most likely to be thinking about leaving their jobs. The issue remains top-five until you get to workers 55 and above—where it falls out of pole position. This showcases a powerful disconnect—the issue most relevant to the younger workers most at risk of attrition isn't on the radar of the older group best represented in C-suites and boards.

What does all of this tell us? First, it reinforces the core idea behind conducting employee listening efforts: don't assume; *ask*. If groups in your organization have dramatically different reasons for becoming disengaged and leaving, you'd want to know the full array of reasons and not risk just "saving" one group or another. Second, it shows how organizations that generally aim to be equitable (which is the vast majority of organizations today) still struggle to create equitable impacts. This is why it's critical to consider the impacts of seemingly neutral policies, procedures, processes, and decisions, not just the intentions. Finally, it underscores the need to not "spread the peanut butter thin" when considering how to create the best possible employee experience; if certain groups have deeper needs, dig in there. Trying to make everyone sort of happy may be a recipe for hemorrhaging the talent you actually need.

In this chapter so far, we've looked at an array of experiences across the workforce that may be driving attrition. But what about the folks you "hired" by accident? Another key area to drive more intentional workforce thinking, and more efficient and effective work, lies in the realm of the contingent workforce.

Contingency Planning: From Shadow to Intentional Workforces

If I told you 30% to 40% of your workforce was hired without the slightest involvement of HR, that those employees are completely untrained, and that in critical operational parts of your company, they might completely outnumber other employees. . .that would alarm you, right?

Across many organizations, this seemingly troubling state of affairs is the norm.

Welcome to the shadowy, often costly world of unintentional contingent workforces.

Contingent work can be the ultimate double-edged sword. In an ideal world, contingent workers provide much-needed flexibility for organizations, adding critical capacity and capability at just the right time without bogging down long-term cost structures. In this state of the world, contingent workers reap the benefits of flexibility too—doing the work they want, when they want, on their own terms.

However, we often hire contingent workers for less-than-ideal reasons. Managers may reach for contingent workers to evade hiring freezes or headcount caps on permanent talent—effectively gaming the system. This phenomenon plays out at an organizational level too, as companies use contingent labor to play financial and accounting games by keeping formal headcount low or to limit benefits expenditures. As my colleague and HR transformation expert, Karen Piercy, explains, these shell games don't always work so well—and talent gets trapped in "neither here nor there" roles that don't benefit either them or their employer. She describes an organization where "at one point they had a headcount cap and so certain jobs became contract jobs, but they're not temporary jobs. . .they stay there all the time. The people have to cycle out after three years because you can only be a contractor for three years, but the vacancy remains after they leave. So when someone leaves, then someone new comes in that role for three. And the cycle goes on forever!"

Does any of this sound familiar? Many organizations have a version of this phenomenon: temporary contract roles turned permanent filled by a revolving door of contractors, or allegedly temporary contract workers turned longstanding employees. The first case is problematic because no one stays long enough to truly build and deploy institutional knowledge; the second is problematic because workers are de facto institutional knowledge carriers, but lack the resources afforded to "real" (heavy quotes there) permanent employees. In each case, organizations destroy value by obscuring the relationship between employees and the real nature of the work they do—setting up resource challenges where they don't need to exist. Part of the challenge is a deep mindset that treats contractors like transactional assets, in contrast to permanent employees where the organization seeks to build a deeper relationship. This way of thinking shortchanges what can be a fantastic talent pool: when my colleagues in Mercer's Workforce Strategy and Analytics group analyzed actual employee data for one large organization, they found that contractors who became full-time employees ended up having both higher performance ratings and higher retention rates than campus hires.

Challenges in managing contract work don't always stem from headcount gamesmanship, though. Contingent workers are sometimes called in to do misunderstood work when managers are self-aware enough to understand that they *don't* know what they're hiring for—and temporary talent seems a lower-risk way to get the work done. This particular move has both positive and negative consequences. On the negative side, the sort of emerging capability that contingent talent often gets deployed against is often a source of strategic advantage and quickly becomes a mainstream, core capability as markets evolve. It's counterintuitive to have workers with whom your organization has a looser connection doing your most important work. That said, remember the whole process we looked at as to why it's hard to hire folks for new kinds of work? Everything from the process of "cloning" job requisitions to trying to navigate rounds of hiring interviews conducted by folks who may not understand emerging categories of work? Well, when organizations utilize contingent talent for new kinds of work, they've done an end run around that entire broken process. Look at it through that lens, and there's something sneakily brilliant about using contractors for emergent, misunderstood work—especially since people who seek out contract work often show high levels of agility and can frame the work better even as they're doing it. Organizations have to be careful, though—if your highest agility employees are going to be managed by Procurement (again, the group that often hires contract workers), you better have one heck of a Procurement department.

Compounding these problems is the fact that regulation designed to protect contingent workers generates unintended negative consequences for employer and employee alike. Most prominently, laws mandating that any worker offered a certain level of training becomes a legal FTE can keep companies from offering contingent workers sufficient training, lest they accidentally take these workers onto the payroll formally.[3]

Under these circumstances, the working experience of contingent workers can be the very opposite of empowering. Many struggle to "get enough hours" to earn a living wage, and the absence of benefits in these roles can be financially ruinous if a health crisis occurs. Their connection to mainstream employee experience can be tenuous, nonexistent, or downright negative. For instance, stories abound of contractors being physically separated from other employees, which can have a negative psychological impact.[4]

Contingent workers live in what students of literature would call a "liminal space"—a place that is neither here nor there. This sounds ethereal until you look at them from the point of view of either Human Resources or, critically, Finance. These workers are often hired by Procurement and lurk just outside the organization's systems. In a best-case scenario, they're actually in the organization's HRIS (generally at a fraction of the license cost of full-time workers), but often no record exists within the organization of their names or even the exact number of them working at any given time. Contractors are tracked financially in systems distinct from other workers, and the spend on their work is often managed separately too.

Alarmingly, as well, the mainstream versus contract workforces have different characteristics. I'll quote a study from the Aspen Institute that shows these disparities in the tech workforce quite starkly:[5]

- Contract workers receive fewer benefits than direct tech workers.

- People of color are overrepresented in contract roles compared to the overall tech workforce.

- Contract workers of color are more likely to be paid hourly than annually and to receive lower pay than White contract workers.

- Contract workers of color are less likely to be converted to direct employment than White contract workers.

—The Aspen Institute

Echoing themes from throughout this chapter, contract workers are often people with demographic differences who end up experiencing work very differently—a situation worth remedying thoughtfully if your organization wants to transform the people systems of how work and pay are organized for the future. Making your workforce intentional—one that works for *all* populations *and* the business outcomes you're seeking—is a critical first step toward actually achieving the future of work and not just talking about it.

We've looked at varying experiences of workers across demographic groups and worker types. So now let's turn the lens in the other direction: how we look at the performance of each individual. It turns out that an area where organizations put a great amount of effort into intentionally creating workforce outcomes is in fact generating a strong proportion of unintended consequences. And it could be because the very origins of performance management are a bit dark.

Maximizing Human Assets: The Disturbing History of Individual Performance Management

We often think about how we manage individuals as a holdover from the management theories practiced during the Industrial Revolution—the "man as machine" thinking of "scientific management" advocates like Frederick Taylor.

The truth is worse. Performance management, as practiced today with the very best of intentions across millions of organizations, is largely derived from the management science of slaveholding. As an array of historians, including the 1619 Project, have uncovered, the very notion of looking at and measuring individual impact on work in quantifiable ways was developed by slaveowners to maximize the productivity of their human "assets."

In her book, *Accounting for Slavery: Masters and Management*, historian Caitlin Rosenthal details how, as more and more slaveowners relied on others to manage their plantations, those slaveholders developed elaborate systems to measure and influence slave workers' outputs. What we think of as neutral practices, like recording the output of workers and measuring them against each other, were in fact developed specific to the context of needing to manage slaves, often from afar as many owners moved back to England. Particularly chilling is Rosenthal's account of how plantation owners used their incredible control over slaves' lives to "test and learn" how human factors, like how long women breastfed their babies, had an impact on their production.[6] We can decry these practices all we want, but their echoes persist. Consider the fact that maternity leave periods are remarkably consistent across organizations (often 16 weeks). We're still making some inhuman connections there between the amount of care for a child and worker productivity.

Furthermore, as Mercer research has shown repeatedly,[7] how organizations measure individual performance can be susceptible to an array of outside factors, yielding individual results that then shouldn't be used as a basis for decision-making. Our Workforce Analytics practitioners have conducted detailed statistical analysis on performance ratings at an array of organizations, and time after time, holding all else equal, we observe factors other than the actual quality of results produced by an individual driving underlying performance ratings and promotion decisions:

- At one consumer goods organization, the deepest driver of performance ratings was whether you worked for the U.S. division or the global one.

- At a financial services firm, everything from the size and demographics of your team to how highly rated your supervisor was drove performance ratings more than actual individual results did.

- At a retail company, an array of factors (again ranging from your functional role to your tenure to your supervisor's rating) meaningfully impacted women's ability to get promoted, but the same factors barely affected men's.

- At a technology company, all factors being held equal, older workers received lower performance ratings—a phenomenon we see consistently across an array of organizations. This finding is ironic because often analysis of the relationship between business results and demographic factors demonstrates that older workers drive the majority of productivity in a given business unit, as we observed in work with a major natural resources company.

In short, thoughtful quantitative analysis shows that performance data are incredibly noisy at best and downright biased at worst. While the Mercer research makes these effects incredibly clear, an array of research has demonstrated similar phenomena.

These data on performance management, as with much of the data on variations in workforce experience across this chapter, is genuinely alarming. We hold performance management up as a cornerstone of how we drive everything from day-to-day productivity to short- or long-term growth. If we're not properly connecting outcomes to performance measures, a host of core business assumptions could be off. Luckily, there are areas where organizations can focus to begin to address the problems uncovered by an evidence-driven examination of how we hire and manage workforces.

What to Do: Organization Level

- **Strategy 51: Rigorously and regularly audit your performance management results for bias—and be prepared to take dramatic action to address.** Diversity, equity, and inclusion thinking within organizations is evolving, rightfully, from examining fairness of process to evaluating whether equity of outcomes is actually achieved. Many organizations' performance management processes pass muster under the former paradigm—they're free of visible bias in the process itself—but fail dramatically under the latter. As we saw in the examples earlier in the chapter, performance management results can be knocked off a fair course by biases centering on everything from demographics to role to geography to external market conditions to one's supervisor's own performance. Getting "under the hood" each and every performance management cycle (including the more real-time efforts of some organizations) is the only way to course correct on these biases when it matters. But to actually address bias issues, organizations may have to take what feel like very stark actions. Examples of these stark actions might include getting rid of higher rankings (or limiting them to particular, nonrecurring scenarios), completely severing the link between pay and performance (an oft-debated tactic), or doing away with certain kinds of qualitative feedback. While seemingly aggressive, these tactics may sweep away either bias, or the impact of bias, for large populations.

- **Strategy 52: Cultivate thoughtful ways of managing performance by team or unit, avoiding the "hand-to-hand combat" of measuring individual by individual.** At the executive level, organizations tend to align incentives in team form pretty decently, often compensating C-suite leaders or their direct reports on overall firm, functional, divisional, or geographic performance to avoid the "balloon squeezing" that results when a company unit is encouraged to pump up their results to the direct detriment of another unit. Below executive level, though, performance measurement by team often falls apart pretty quickly, with everyone below a fairly high level of leadership measured as individuals and then a collection of individuals—not as a team or a system.

- **Strategy 53: Bring your contingent workforce up to "measurement parity" with your full-time workforce,**

including shared governance, capture in organizational systems, and centralized budgeting. When it comes to contingent workforces, the old adage "can't measure, can't manage" has never been truer. My colleague, Karen Piercy, an HR transformation expert, notes the financial disconnect that arises as unintentional contingent workforces get larger and larger: "Clients started asking questions like, *Well, wait, if the third of my workforce is contingent and I'm the head of comp, but I don't know what we pay out for that. That doesn't make any sense. That's a labor cost that we're not managing in HR as a labor cost. We're managing it as an expense somewhere else.*" Close collaboration between HR and Procurement is critical here, including a single-system and financially unified view of the workforce, across all worker types.

- **Strategy 54: Rigorously and regularly audit your pay philosophy and pay equity—are you paying for what you think you're paying for, and are you paying fairly in real time?** Per Mercer's Global Talent Trends 2022 research, only one in three organizations have a compensation philosophy that states pay should be both externally competitive and internally consistent. A similar percentage—28%—are both offering a wider variety of reward types and proactively adjusting compensation to create better internal equity. These leading-practice ways of operating, which many employees would honestly view as cost of entry, will increasingly make this roughly one-third of employers far more attractive talent destinations than the two-thirds of organizations that haven't refreshed how they look at rewards. Taking a quantitatively rigorous and regularly refreshed look at topics like pay philosophy and pay equity also avoids a periodic panic around the compensation "arms races" that we see in markets ranging from actuaries to physician's assistants to warehouse workers. Pay equity, especially, must be refreshed yearly because in fast-moving talent markets new hires regularly knock previously established equitable pay out of joint.[8]

- **Strategy 55: Figure out which employee groups are "burnt out," and which are "fed up," and design differentiated strategies to address each set of issues.** Savvy employee listening, including newer strategies such as digital focus groups incorporating up to 1,000 employees or ethnographic surveys that capture how employees feel about particular components of their work at various points in the day, can help organizations identify which groups are "burnt out" (frustrated with excess workload at a given point) and which are "fed up" (wrestling with deep frustration about structural aspects of their job, such as compensation, intensified work, or both, that have been problematic for a long time). "Burnt out" employees require more short-term and more traditional wellness strategies—improved benefits, temporary reprieves from work such as company-wide days off, etc. To care for "fed up" employees, organizations must deploy a completely different set of strategies—reorganizing work or rethinking compensation structures (particularly for long-suffering hourly workers). Knowing who falls into which group is critical to getting the journey right.

What to Do: Team Level

Further good news: even at the team level, you can take concrete actions to make sure your workforce, at miniature scale, is hired and managed more intentionally and equitably.

- **Strategy 56: Confront your contractor addiction.** Are 1099s piling up at your team's door, metaphorically speaking? It's worth taking a searching look at how, when, and why your team hires contractors—as well as what work they do and how long they stick around. You can't solve for organization-level contingent workforce issues at the team level, but you can move from "part of the problem" to "part of the solution." To really have impact, these conversations should be contextualized to broader discussions about what work the team takes on, how that work gets done, and how the team works together. You may find, for instance, that you've established excellent psychological safety among full-time employees, but operate under a complete culture of fear for your contingent workers, who live in terror of being cut off for a single mistake. Alternatively, you may find that work is sensibly segmented and distributed among 1099 employees, but that your full-time team members are swimming through a soup of undefined work and unclear tasks. Either way, unless you ask, you won't have the opportunity to move to a more effective way of operating.

- **Strategy 57: Regularly unpack the work/reward balance for your team, and teach them how to do the same for their teams—in real-time, not just at year-end.** During the Great Resignation, I've had the opportunity to connect with a number of groups that focus on compensation and rewards for their organizations. In these conversations, we always end up talking about the same idea: that the worst thing that can happen to organizations in highly competitive labor markets is for workers to say, "You can't pay me enough to do this job!" Once workers have hit that point, an entire range of options for retention, the pay side of the scale, is gone. You can certainly make changes to working environments, but those changes often take longer to act on, and the clock may run out as workers are snapped up by rapacious talent competitors. To avoid this sort of crisis, leaders must create an open and ongoing dialogue about how well-rewarded their teams feel—and equip their direct reports to cascade that conversation all the way down to the front line. Historically, managers have been loathe to engage on this subject, fearing a "Pandora's box effect" where dissatisfaction is stirred up by the very mention of work versus reward. But in today's market, where sites like Glassdoor make the basics of compensation and work experience fully transparent, one can consider the subject permanently up for discussion. In this context, it's better to engage, listen, and find a solution than to get caught out as critical talent walks out the door.

- **Strategy 58: Identify your "talent competitors," especially those who are not your business competitors.** It's a bit of a cliché that as all companies' work becomes more technology-inflicted, every company is competing with the tech giants for critical talent. Unfortunately, it's also true—and this effect has been magnified massively by a "work from anywhere" world where location-agnostic jobs continue to increase in prevalence. When Mercer's Workforce Strategy and Analytics group performs external labor market analyses for clients, we routinely find both positive and negative surprises on the availability of talent locally. Knowing whom you're competing with for talent—and understanding how those organizations balance the experience of work with appropriate rewards—can inform far smarter talent attraction and retention strategies. And as we'll discuss further in Chapter 7, the talent you need may be even closer to home than you think. Mercer's head of Mobility, Taryn Kramer, notes that during the pandemic and associated talent shortages, companies "had to look inward and really focus more on what talent do they have in a particular location, or how can we develop the talent that we have already to focus more on learning and development opportunities to build their capabilities or develop skills versus bringing that in from an external resource." That's right—you may need to be hiring from. . .yourself.

- **Strategy 59: Rigorously train on bias before *each* performance management cycle.** At this point in the chapter, you may be feeling pretty bleak about performance management. And that would be a fair feeling! But you may also be thinking, "Gosh, it would be great to just chuck our performance management processes out the window, but that's not possible right now." And that's organizational reality at many, many organizations. So what can you do? Here's a simple thought: train for unconscious bias *right before each performance management cycle.* Research conducted by Mercer's Workforce Strategy and Analytics group showed that when bias training happened in the few months before performance management processes took place, bias in the results was reduced meaningfully. When the training was at a greater time remove from the process, the effect went away. . .arguing for unconscious bias training to be repeated just before each performance management cycle so that the concepts are truly fresh in leaders' minds and actually get used.

- **Strategy 60: Embed "everyday workforce analytics" into how you and the team work.** There's a strong case for sophisticated workforce analytics, to be sure, and many of the interesting and provocative findings highlighted in this chapter come from these methods as deployed by Mercer's Workforce Analytics team. That said, workforce analytics is a game everyone can play—and not just HR either. Embedding sensible people analytics into everyday decision-making can be a powerful engine for better team performance. Use data to question your assumptions: for instance, do team members who log more hours over-perform on business metrics as a result, or have their seemingly less-hard-working colleagues actually cracked the code on an efficient way of operating that ultimately yields better results? These simple inquiries often don't require anything fancier than Excel and a couple of folks who are truly close to the underlying data sets. Making decisions this way creates a true spirit of fairness and will often lead to unexpected sources of value.

Thinking differently about working populations and intentional workforces will certainly speed up the journey to the future of work for many organizations. As we'll see in Chapter 7, there are three workforce-level issues—immigration, migration, and incarceration—that bear particular scrutiny, as their potential and current impacts are far-ranging.

7 Hippos Under the Lagoon

The Powerful Effects of Immigration, Migration, and Incarceration on Your Workforce

"We asked for workers. We got people instead."

—Max Frisch

The most dangerous animal in Africa is a plant-eater perhaps best known for wearing tutus in a long-ago Disney cartoon. That's right: hippos kill more people every year than lions. There are a few reasons why they're so deadly, including a territorial attitude and surprisingly large, sharp teeth, but the most interesting one doesn't have to do with any of their characteristics—it has to do with where they hang out. Hippos spend a lot of time in rivers and lakes, so a pretty good proportion of the folks killed by them don't see them coming as they emerge, angry, from underneath a boat.

We spend a lot of time on workforce issues analogous to lions: visible predators stalking the savannah. This chapter, though, deals with three "hippo" issues—immigration, migration, and incarceration—that lurk beneath the surface of organization's workforces. We'll examine how these issues reshape workforces and how a more human approach to grappling with all three forces can be a tremendous source of productivity and improved employee experience for organizations.

Why do these issues qualify as true "hippos"? All three have a direct impact on two of the absolutely seminal workforce issues of our time: labor shortages and creating a more inclusive, diverse workforce. At Mercer, we believe that the current labor shortage—where job listings outnumber unemployed workers by 5 million[1]—is structural in nature and likely to worsen, turning today's Great Resignation from a temporary virus into a chronic illness, the "long COVID-19" of labor markets. As we'll see in this chapter, constructively orienting your organization on the issues of immigration, migration, and incarceration can actually create labor supply breakthroughs. Similarly, for organizations truly concerned about creating a diverse, inclusive workforce to address everything from diverse consumers to a need for disruptive innovation, making progress on how your organization handles immigration, migration, and incarceration can be a source of game-changing progress, as all three issues have a measurable impact on the diversity of working populations. In short, getting your strategy right on these "hippos" can powerfully differentiate your organization as a truly human place to work and create the workforce stability and impact needed to thrive in an increasingly complicated future.

To understand the *how* and *why* of these three key issues, let's start by examining immigration. Please note, for simplicity's sake we'll be using U.S. law and statistics in this chapter, but the underlying dynamics play out in many ways in virtually every country in the world.

I'm Not Going to Quote Hamilton But Immigrants Really Do Play a Crucial Role in the American Workforce

According to the Bureau of Labor Statistics, foreign-born workers make up about 17% of the American workforce, or slightly more than one in six workers.[2] Analysts have seen a drop in immigration due to COVID-19 and stricter federal policies as a force exacerbating the current labor shortage, especially in industries such as hospitality and food service that rely heavily on workers from abroad.[3]

To understand the immigration issue in the workforce context, let's start with where foreign-born labor plays an essential role. Interestingly, the category where we see the highest proportion of foreign-born workers is private households rather than organizations—fully 45% of workers in this category are born outside the United States, split pretty evenly between authorized and unauthorized immigration status.[4] You may hear that statistic and say, oh, well, not my organization's problem—but in fact, this is the group that provides the childcare and other supportive services that keep the rest of the labor force at work. In some ways, this group's work could be considered foundational to the smooth running of the entire economy; as we've seen during the COVID-19 period, childcare failures set off a set of dominoes that threaten to keep women out of the workforce entirely. Moreover, the hoary cliché about immigrants taking on work judged unappealing by native-born workers also plays out in the data. Immigrants take on a high proportion of dangerous and deadly jobs: when you examine the top occupational areas populated by foreign-born workers, which include farming/fishing/forestry and construction/extraction, you see meaningful overlap with the jobs we talked about in Chapter 1 where you have a higher proportion of dying at work. Finally, if it wasn't for foreign-born labor, we wouldn't eat: immigrant populations represent 33% of workers in agriculture, 29% in food manufacturing, and looking at occupational category rather than industry, 22% of the workers in food preparation.[5]

Now, you might still be looking at all of this and saying, very interesting for society, but I'm still not getting why this matters to my workplace. To bring the immigration topic to pragmatic, organizational level, let's look at three different use cases:

- First-generation foreign-born workers who are citizens or "green card" holders

- Foreign-born workers who are in a particular country on visas for "high-skills" or "low-skills" workers (we'll discuss the use of quote marks shortly)

- Foreign-born workers who are underemployed, doing work less complex than the work they trained to do in their countries of origin

The Massive Diversity, Equity, and Inclusion Issue You're Not Focused On: Foreign-Born Workers Who Are Citizens or "Green Card" Holders

Pew Center data shows that 72% of immigrants in the United States are either naturalized citizens or "green card" holders with most of the rights of citizenship (Figure 7.1).[6] Assuming that percentage roughly carries through to the 17% of the overall workforce composed of foreign-born workers, that means about one in eight people in your employee population was born outside the United States but is now a U.S. citizen or green card holder. Allowing for intersectionality between the two populations as a matter of course, that's a proportion similar to the percentage of Black employees in the workforce. It's a lot of folks and worth caring about.

For foreign-born workers who are citizens or green card holders, the "one key workforce issue" can be summarized in a single word:

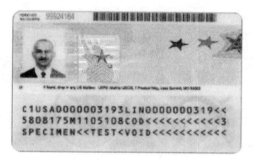

Figure 7.1   A U.S. "Green Card"

Source: USCIS / Wikimedia Commons / Public Domain.

microaggressions. A 2015 *Vox* article defines microaggressions as "the kinds of remarks, questions, or actions that are painful because they have to do with a person's membership in a group that's discriminated against or subject to stereotypes."[7] Microaggressions may sound small, but in fact they quickly add up to "death by a thousand cuts," both exhausting the people repeatedly exposed to them and ultimately blocking their progress just as surely as open and large-scale discrimination would.

For foreign-born workers who are citizens or green card holders, microaggressions might include the following:

- Being asked if you are in the country legally
- Being asked why your English is so good

- Others trying to imitate your accent

- Being subjected to stereotypes, positive or negative, about your country of origin (for example, "Oh, you guys are all good at technology work.")

- Being told your behavior is somehow atypical for your country of origin (for example, "You're way more vocal than I'd expect for someone from. . .")

- Being asked where you're "really from"

- Others assuming you do particular work because you're from a particular country

- Having your experience invalidated (for example, "From what I've seen, this company is 100% a meritocracy.")

- Insensitivity to the language and traditions of your country of origin (A 2015 article in *The Atlantic* features an excruciating example of this, where the writer of the article was told by a fellow student that the writer's name was also the name of that student's dog.[8])

- Having your name mispronounced or misspelled. Repeatedly.

Do you feel tired reading that list? Imagine living it, or perhaps you already do. The day-to-day experience of foreign-born workers has, in general, been a laggard area for diversity, equity, and inclusion efforts for organizations, who've struggled to triage among other dire workforce needs. As workforce DEI efforts evolve, though, focusing on the needs of foreign-born workers will become more critical for two reasons. First, this is a large and heretofore virtually unattended-to population. As labor shortages continue, efforts to improve the day-to-day experience of these workers have the potential for large-scale impact on retention, both bringing down hiring costs and maximizing the productivity of highly skilled populations. Second, efforts to help these populations are highly synergistic to existing DEI efforts, due to immigration status being yet another card in the stacked deck of intersectionality. Imagine the experience of a White male foreign-born worker from an English-speaking country versus that of a Black female foreign-born worker from a non-English-speaking country. The former employee likely suffers far fewer microaggressions than the latter employee. Elevate the experience for foreign-born workers overall, and the impact of your overall DEI efforts is bound to increase.

Working in Limbo: The Unique Travails of Foreign-Born Workers on Visas

Your organization may consider itself already an expert on visas for foreign-born workers. Pre-pandemic, the U.S. government issued about 2 million visas per year, though this number fell dramatically during COVID-19 and as a consequence of the federal government's more jaundiced view on the benefits of immigration.[9] For companies from high tech to Big Agriculture, navigating visa processes from a legal perspective is part of doing business. Critical work could not be done without the labor of visa holders; one fabulous example is provided by the American Immigration Council, who note that "over the past decade (FY 2010–FY 2019), eight companies that were developing a coronavirus vaccine—Gilead Sciences, Moderna Therapeutics, GlaxoSmithKline, Inovio, Johnson & Johnson Pharmaceuticals, Regeneron, Vir Therapeutics, and Sanofi—received approvals for 3,310 biochemists, biophysicists, chemists, and other scientists through the H-1B program."[10] Accordingly, many companies have over time become quite proficient at navigating the legal and bureaucratic labyrinth required to get employees working legally in the United States.

Just because you're good at getting the forms filled out, though, doesn't mean your company is sensibly managing the experience of visa-holders. The legal work is "necessary but not sufficient," and the employee experience of working on a visa can often be quite challenging, in ways that impact employee mental health and thus productivity—hitting your bottom line and creating ethics issues alike.

Let's dive into the unseen swirl of issues around employees working on visas. But first it's important to note that while we hear about H-1Bs all of the time, those are just one visa type, and each has their own nuances. From L visas that allow for internal international transfers to seasonal-worker visas that allow employees into the country for the duration of a harvest season, specifics vary meaningfully. Employers need to think through the second- and third-order impacts of the visa types their particular employees are on.

That said, when we consider the employee experience of being on a visa, there are three overall places where it glitches out—all of which impact both that worker's individual wellness and what they are able to accomplish for the organization:

- **You're pretty much tied to your current employer.** For the vast majority of the working world, as employers we make decisions believing employees can pick up and go get another job if they don't like the one they have. Visa-holders can't do this—in most cases, they're tied to the company sponsoring their visa for some period or another. This is a feature of the visa system, not a bug: the underlying assumption of a government-issued visa is that the sponsoring organization has a unique need that can't be filled by talent born in that country, and thus a visa can't be framed initially as an invitation to work fungibly across any job in a given country. As reasonable as this notion is in the abstract, though, in practice it can lead to questionable behavior by employers who don't have to feel the influence of competitive talent markets. "Where are they gonna go?" can become an unfortunate catch-phrase for decisions around everything from pay to career advancement to the content of work. Visa-holders aren't blind to this way of thinking, and I've heard countless stories of this group tolerating intolerable things (like abusive supervisors or bizarrely constructed work) because. . . "Where are they gonna go?" Tolerating poor working conditions due to feeling trapped is obviously painful for these workers, but it also hits your organization's bottom line, as factors like abusive supervision have been shown to negatively correlate with productivity.[11]

- **Your travel is restricted, making interactions with your social support network difficult.** One interesting facet of the visa process that stretches far outside the office is the restrictions on travel it places. Depending on what kind of visa you're working under, as a visa-holder you may not be able to travel back to your country of origin at all, you may be able to travel a limited amount, or you may be able to travel freely, but with tremendous bureaucratic burden attached. Even before the increased travel restrictions that came with COVID-19, reduced or eliminated travel home was a meaningful source of stress for individuals who were limited in their ability to see aging parents, extended family and friends, or even children left behind with relatives or other caregivers. For visa-holding employees, being distanced from loved ones can be a constant source of stress humming in the background, rarely articulated to their employer but palpably affecting their mental health and ability to contribute to their full potential.

- **You work under great uncertainty with rules that change often (including your company's!).** Because regulatory change can happen at any time, and a large number of factors can cause visa processes to slow down or speed up, visa-holders live with a degree of day-to-day uncertainty that can also create a tremendous mental burden. To some degree, they live at minor risk of being thrown out of the country they live and work in—every day! Their ability to plan simple life choices is inhibited by far-away bureaucratic gyrations, and even the best-intentioned governments can behave irrationally. I'll never forget a funny and benign example of this phenomenon: when I worked as a visa-holder in the United Kingdom, our visas were stamped with the phrase "no recourse to public funds." A coworker of mine, on the same visa, had a baby while we were working there, and the government promptly started mailing him checks every month, which looked suspiciously like "public funds"! Under a rubric like that, it's hard to count on even very basic assumptions about how the visa process will run.

All in all, working as a visa-holder presents a unique, and often emotionally destabilizing, day-to-day employee experience. As we'll discuss later in this chapter, employers need to be careful to both care for this group properly and avoid accidentally exploitative behaviors. If organizations took a more active role to support the wellness of this group, their already impressive economic contributions could increase even further.

Doctors Driving Taxis Amid a Healthcare Shortage: The Continuing Puzzle of Immigrant Underemployment

If you've lived in New York City long enough, you've been in a cab driven by a foreign-born worker with an advanced degree. As we continue to stare down the barrel of pervasive labor shortages, this always-disturbing phenomenon looks even worse than it did historically. Research from the Migration Policy Institute suggests that 21% of college-educated immigrants are underemployed, either not working or working at jobs that only require a high school education.[12] It's worth noting that 16% of college graduates who are born within the United States suffer from the same phenomenon, so while the 21% statistic is scary, it's best to think of it as "measurably more likely to be underemployed than a person born in the United States." Which is still terrible, to be sure.

What drives underemployment among foreign-born workers? MPI researchers cite simple things: baseline bias against Black and Hispanic workers, lack of English proficiency, nontransferrable foreign credentials in technical areas like medicine, and legal immigration status.[13] Of these areas, the transferability of credentials is least under employers' control, while English proficiency is comparably easy to address. Organizations often neglect English-language training as a way of sourcing talent previously untapped in the market, especially for roles that are becoming increasingly "impossible to hire for."

In short, foreign-born workers are a crucial segment of the labor market who don't, generally, receive the support they deserve. Immigration-aware policies and smart sourcing of this population can be critical weapons in the war for talent.

Work from Anywhere? The Migration Question

We've examined some areas to address to increase the impact of, and experience for, foreign-born workers. But what about those folks who move around within the same country?

A robust discussion of flexibility at work encompasses all of the dimensions you might have learned about at your high school newspaper—who, what, when, where, why, and how—but over the last few years during the pandemic, companies have particularly obsessed over a single dimension: where. Are workers going to truly disperse across the United States, and indeed the world, given greater ability to "work from anywhere"? Or will we slowly amble back into offices and the cities around them?

Let's start by looking at the data and busting some myths.

Myth 1: Patterns of labor migration around the Great Resignation are
   unprecedented.

Reality 1: This isn't the first time workers got fed up and moved.

There's no disputing the data: during the Great Resignation,
workers have reset on what they value. Mercer's 2022 Global Talent
Trends survey showed what data said: the rhetoric around
"unprecedented" movements around the country is without question
excess hype. Certainly, Americans are moving: data from moving
services provider North American shows that in 2021, people moved
from high cost of living states (Illinois, California, New Jersey,
Michigan, New York) to lower cost of living states (South Carolina,
Idaho, Tennessee, North Carolina, Florida, Arizona, Texas). By their
estimates, more Americans are moving too—20% more in 2021 than
in 2020.[14]

That said, the notion that the United States is experiencing an
unprecedented amount of migration due to remote work is flawed on
two fronts. First, the amounts of pandemic-era migration remain
"relatively modest" per U.S. Census data.[15] Interestingly, the Census
analysis notes that migration patterns offset what would have been
population declines across most of the counties in the country; while
73% of counties had more births than deaths, 58% ended the year
with more people than they had before due to migration. Taken in
this light, migration in the pandemic period looks more like a
periodic systemic rebalancing than a linear, permanent trend.

Moreover, as Twitter wags are fond of saying regarding any
number of things, "This is actually precedented." Between 1916 and
1970, more than 6 million Blacks left the South in search of both
better pay and working conditions and a way of life where
discrimination and abuse were not thoroughly pervasive.[16] The
bravery and impact of this group's actions are not to be
underestimated: everything from the Harlem Renaissance to the

increasing industrialization of the United States can be traced to this group's decision to "vote with their feet." It was a social commentary with profound economic resonance; as John Dollard, an anthropologist, noted, "Oftentimes, just to go away is one of the most aggressive things that another person can do."[17]

To learn more about the Great Migration, I highly recommend Isabel Wilkerson's wonderful 2011 book, *The Warmth of Other Suns: The Epic Story of America's Great Migration,* which tells the story of this incredible social movement through the lens of a handful of individuals' stories. For organizations, it's worth looking at what conditions might prompt another Great Migration, or miniature versions thereof—are there areas where the treatment of a particular group is so miserable that that group might actually migrate out?

Myth 2: Major cities are dead.

Reality 2: Cities ebb and flow, perennially.

The headlines have been incessant: Will the rise of "work from anywhere" decimate the cities? In 5 years, will we all be working from our respective porches in our respective small towns?

When we look at the data, this seems unlikely. First, similar to the prior myth, longer-run data shows a pattern of workers moving in and out of cities. Per the Brookings Institution, the largest 10% of metro areas in the U.S. share of workers has bounced around from about 50% to nearly 54% from 1979 to 2019, hitting a low in 1995 and a high just pre-pandemic. In fact, from 2011 to 2019, worker concentration in the largest cities had risen each year, consistently.[18] Why does this pre-pandemic uptick matter? Perhaps because it positions workers' movements out of the cities during the pandemic in a different light. If movement into the largest cities had been progressing at a velocity not seen in prior decades, inevitably a certain proportion of those workers would have been drawn into cities more by an overall trend among their peers than deep personal preference. In conditions of adversity, this ambivalent population would of course decamp, but the change is again more a natural rebalancing than large-scale city flight. See Figure 7.2.

Myth 3: Companies dictate the flow of workers as they move their operations around.

Reality 3: Today, workers often control the movements of companies as they migrate.

Conventional wisdom has it that when companies make changes in where they operate, workers are forced to move or face ruin. I'll never forget one of my business school professors ruminating sadly on a suicide among his direct reports when the company decided to move operations from New York to Florida. And indeed, the closing of industrial plants did, over the second part of the twentieth century,

Figure 7.2   New York is pretty charming

decimate many an American city. For instance, Dayton, Ohio, lost 50% of its population between 1960 and today, and another one-third of its population are now below the poverty line.[19]

Today's world of labor mobility looks very different, though. While companies continue to shift and expand where they operate, sometimes in search of tax incentives or simply lower-cost locations, often the primary driving force in their actions is to be where the action is. And by the action, I mean the talent.

For instance, as John Deere moves toward a future of autonomous tractors, new locations in Chicago[20] and Austin[21] will play critical roles in helping the company attract tech talent not available in its traditional Moline, Illinois, hub. As these examples illustrate, the search for tech workers has extended far beyond traditional hubs in Silicon Valley or New York City—the Brookings Institution in fact identifies a whole range of emerging cluster cities for tech talent (Atlanta; Dallas; Denver; Miami; Orlando; San Diego; Kansas City, MO; St. Louis; and Salt Lake City) that represent in aggregate 16% of U.S. tech job listings.[22] Similarly, Google's decision to expand into Atlanta[23] represents a further iteration of this thinking—moving to a city where diverse *tech* talent is already located.

Thinking creatively about talent sources isn't just about geographical moves, though. In the next part of this chapter, we'll address a working population you may not have thought about—but should.

From Prison to Productivity: Why You Should Hire Formerly Incarcerated People

Martha Stewart. Wesley Snipes. Tim Allen. Steve Madden.

What do these celebrities all have in common? They went to prison and then went back to work.

For the average citizen, it's not that simple. Formerly incarcerated people have a 27% unemployment rate, a several-times multiple of the rate among the general population (at the time of the writing of this book, around 4%).[24] This cost is not trivial—economists believe that the economy bleeds between $78 and $87 *billion* a year due to formerly incarcerated people not working.[25]

And of course, similar to what we saw in the data about foreign-born workers, the burden of unemployment is borne disproportionately by formerly incarcerated people who manifest other dimensions of diversity, such as women and Black people.[26]

Back to the eternal question of this chapter: Okay, that's what's happening in the world, why should my organization care? There's actually a straightforward answer on this one—in a world of ever-tightening labor markets, formerly incarcerated people are actually terrific hires, per both data and some blue-chip organizations' case studies. Let's explore why your talent pipeline, just maybe, should be coming from the local prison:

- *They're not actually risky talent.* For more than 20 years, 5% of Johns Hopkins' Health System and Hospitals hires have been formerly incarcerated people—and on performance evaluations, they perform similarly to the other 95% of the population. Moreover, not a single employee in this group has had to be fired for problematic behavior.[27] JP Morgan now hires thousands of people with criminal records as well and has been publicly vocal regarding the success of this policy.[28]

- *They're more loyal employees.* Academic research suggests that formerly incarcerated employees have longer tenures and are less likely to quit voluntarily than other workers.[29] Johns Hopkins' hiring program has observed this effect, noting a 43% retention rate—meaningfully better than other workers.[30]

- *They have unique skill sets.* Jennifer Soble, executive director of the Illinois Prison Project, notes that due to the many, many challenges of navigating a prison environment, formerly incarcerated workers often have dramatically higher emotional intelligence than their workplace peers. In a world where "soft skills" trade at an ever higher premium, and hard skills are considered more and more teachable, this hard-won experience is not to be discounted.

What to Do: Organization Level

- **Strategy 61: In your diversity, equity, and inclusion (DEI) efforts, consider a broader array of populations, including foreign-born workers, previously incarcerated populations, etc.** To date, companies' efforts in the DEI realm have, by necessity, focused on groups that remain meaningfully under-represented in many key roles and whose input is still not fulsomely considered in many aspects of corporate culture: women and ethnic/racially diverse individuals. These groups will, and should, remain a major focus for organizations; as long as we see a dearth of women and ethnic and racially diverse individuals in positions of leadership, we need to continue to solve very basic issues for these large groups. That said, broadening the DEI lens to include groups like foreign-born workers or previously incarcerated people can yield tremendous benefits in terms of improved mental health and thus productivity, or accessing previously untapped skill sets. Moreover, due to meaningful intersectionality between these populations and the groups more classically addressed by DEI efforts, anything you do to bolster the position of these groups within your workforce will elevate your existing DEI initiatives.

- **Strategy 62: Dramatically up the inclusion factor on your talent acquisition process.** Remember the data from Chapter 4 about how organizations spend three times as much time on talent acquisition as talent management? With that allocation of time and resources, it's worth getting talent acquisition really right. As we've seen in this chapter, to combat the Great Resignation by really taking advantage of labor markets in the broadest sense (including populations like underemployed foreign-born workers, formerly incarcerated people, or geographically mobile talent), fundamental aspects of talent acquisition need to shift. Areas for change might include where talent is sourced, what support is provided in the interview process, or what operates as a "disqualifier" (prison record, poor English, no college, etc.). Reconsider the very fundamentals of how you hire workers: decisions that seemed obvious in looser labor markets may make filling key roles impossible under long-run labor shortages. Questioning your assumptions using some of the lenses in this chapter can allow you to source higher-impact talent at lower cost—the ultimate win-win.

- **Strategy 63: Understand the role of foreign-born workers at your organization, including the household workers who support your employees, and actively create support programs for this group (including naturalized/green card workers and workers on visas).** As we've seen in this chapter, foreign-born workers live with a lot of day-to-day trauma in the workplace—everything from microaggressions to ongoing uncertainty as to whether they'll be allowed to stay in the country one more day. There are good, empathic reasons to put more concrete support in place for these workers, and importantly, there is also a strong business case. Mercer's data shows that workers who thrive are more productive *and* sticky to the organization.[31] Moreover, to keep workers' support systems in place, and thus those workers in the workforce, it may make sense to support the foreign-born household workers whose efforts enable them to keep working. . .even up to the point of providing company-driven support to those workers' engagement with legal immigration processes.

- **Strategy 64: Take a searching, quantitative and qualitative look at your remote and hybrid work policies in the context of geographical talent markets, those markets' trends, and with a DEI lens.** In my experience working with C-suites on the remote/hybrid question, these decisions are often emotionally inflected. Executives tend to have a strong view on how their own careers were shaped, and if that narrative emphasizes in-person work or geographical concentration in one location, those beliefs carry through to their views about how their company should operate going forward. In ever-tighter talent markets, though, it's critical that these decisions incorporate real-world evidence on how work flexibility might impact talent attraction and retention— including using a DEI lens. Google's recent decision to open a large Atlanta office is a great example of this sort of decision-making. In this case, company leadership decided that attracting and retaining underrepresented Black talent was worth diffusing populations away from other in-person hubs (Silicon Valley, New York City, etc.). If you're making decisions about location strategy or remote/hybrid work without quantitative reference to talent markets, chances are you're missing a host of opportunities.

- **Strategy 65: Scenario plan your flexibility and location strategy versus possible changes in your talent markets as well as in the way we work.** When asked about his plan to fight Evander Holyfield, Mike Tyson famously said, "Everyone has a plan until they get punched in the mouth."[32] Scenario planning is the best way to think about what happens after that punch. What are the potential disruptors of your location plan? What if a large competitor suddenly goes fully remote? What if a company that hires lots of hourly employees moves into the same town as your biggest plant? What if some of the ways we work fundamentally change—including anything from greater transparency on pay to organizations radically reducing the number of meetings and emphasizing asynchronous work instead? Considering how well your location and flexibility decisions stand up to various types of shocks will help shape a more effective strategy in this regard, even though sometimes that punch to the mouth can't be avoided.

What to Do: Team Level

- **Strategy 66: Drive an ongoing, two-way onboarding journey— especially for diverse or nontraditional hires.** One of the worst things about the onboarding process in general, but especially for hires who have some dimension of diversity, is that it ends. At some point, as organizations we expect folks to be fully assimilated and in the flow of the organization's way of working. There are several problems with these assumptions. First, if you are hired, from a group that is not traditional for the organization (say, formerly incarcerated people) or from a group that has additional mental stressors in the background (say, someone going through a work visa process), your timeline to feel up to speed in the organization may be longer than a more traditional hire's. Second, even for the most mainstream hires, organizations serially underestimate how long it can take to feel comfortable with organizational culture, technology, and processes—especially if that culture, technology, or processes have any degree of complexity. Finally, onboarding should not be a one-way street! The very expectation that when someone joins an organization it is their responsibility to assimilate in certain ways is an antiquated one. In recent years, the notion of "reverse onboarding" has gained ground—where an organization consciously identifies the ways it wants new hires to change them and creates pathways for that to happen.

- **Strategy 67: Incorporate trauma-informed ways of operating.** As Jennifer Soble of the Illinois Prison Project notes, when hiring formerly incarcerated people, it's critical to make sure how they are hired, trained, onboarded, and managed is all trauma-informed. In *Harvard Business Review,* Katharine Manning provides a crisp definition of what it means to be trauma-informed: "Trauma is an emotional injury that affects performance and well-being. . . A trauma-informed organization is one that operates with an understanding of trauma and its negative effects on the organization's employees and the communities it serves and works to mitigate those effects."[33] As Manning notes, due to COVID-19 over the last couple of years, we have all experienced a great deal of trauma. Accordingly, the same principles of trauma-informed operations would help formerly incarcerated people feel psychological safety in the workplace—which according to the CDC include (1) safety; (2) trustworthiness and transparency; (3) peer support; (4) collaboration and mutuality; (5) empowerment, voice, and choice; and (6) cultural, historical, and gender issues.[34] They are in fact helpful to us all as we navigate a working world while dealing with painful recent history and ongoing issues. It's important to remember, too, that trauma is hiding in plain sight all of the time. Recently, a Kentucky court awarded a man $450,000 who was thrown a birthday party at work over his own objections; the party evoked childhood trauma for him.[35] Training supervisors to listen to employees when they cite trauma triggers can be a useful step toward a more psychologically safe working environment.

- **Strategy 68: Cultivate an "immigration aware" mindset— including the foreign-born populations who work in the**

households of your team. In the United States, at least, deeply held beliefs about this country operating as a "melting pot" often lead us to disregard the unique experience of foreign-born workers. As we've seen in this chapter, the population faces unique challenges in working environments—and organizations that take those challenges into account and manage empathically will win the war for a critical talent population. Being immigration-aware should include stamping out microaggressions, providing mental health and practical support for people on visas (above and beyond legal processes), and actively hiring from underemployed foreign-born populations. It's important to think beyond your immediate employees and into the ecosystem that supports them—are there ways you can support the foreign-born workers in their households, say, with access to immigration resources?

- **Strategy 69: Continuously audit your leadership messaging about location in response to changing external and, particularly, labor market conditions.** As conditions have shifted continuously during the pandemic, and indeed continue to shift, leaders have struggled to hit the right notes on where, exactly, employees should be working. Return-to-office campaigns have been stymied by fresh COVID-19 waves and talent populations eyeing row after row of "work from anywhere" job listings. The problem of communicating about location predates COVID-19, though—executives have always faced tough questions about things like the economic impact of headquarters moves. To get the message right, real-time listening to both employees and, frankly, the overall zeitgeist is critical. Whom are you competing for talent with? What messages are they sending? Understanding the overall context your talent is operating in helps reduce the risk of sending messages about location that send key talent running for the hills.

- **Strategy 70: Look at how you can create dimensions of flexibility across whom you hire and how they work.** As my colleague, Lauren Mason, a flexible work guru, is fond of saying, location isn't the only dimension of flexibility—everything from who does a job to when it gets done is up for grabs, if you can be creative enough. Measures like shift flexibility can create true work–life harmony for blue-collar populations that haven't experienced it before. Similarly, breaking open job descriptions and figuring out what's really vital and what's not will help open up the talent lens to a far wider array of folks coming into your organization, including, hopefully, some formerly incarcerated people and some underemployed foreign-born workers.

Coming back to our friends the hippos, we'll end this chapter on a funny note. My colleague, Taryn Kramer, Mercer's head of Mobility, shared with me a story from her childhood in South Africa. Apparently hippos, despite being the most dangerous animal in Africa, also possess an altruistic side. If a crocodile drags humans down into a lake, the herbivore hippos, outraged at the violence, will dive down and pull the crocodiles off—saving the endangered humans. It's the perfect way of thinking about the three "hippo" issues from this chapter—immigration, migration, and incarceration. They're lurking under the water, but properly handled, they can save your organization!

Speaking of saving your organization, in the following chapter we'll dive into two ways organizations endanger themselves: greedy work and *Animal Farm* syndrome. Buckle up and prepare to do some soul-searching.

8 Defeating Greedy Work and *Animal Farm* Syndrome

Two Critical Levers for an Awesome Working Culture

"This work was strictly voluntary, but any animal who absented himself from it would have his rations reduced by half."

—George Orwell, *Animal Farm*

This chapter is, in many ways, the mirror image of the prior chapter. While in the last chapter we explored forces that shape workforces from the outside (immigration, migration, and incarceration), this chapter is all about a couple of forces that impact organizations from within.

The first force, greedy work, could be described colloquially as "the kind of jobs that take over your life." (I'll provide a real definition from a sociologist shortly, don't worry!)

The second force, *Animal Farm* syndrome, describes well-intentioned folks turning into the same bad leaders they once swore they'd never emulate.

Both phenomena can feel insidious and impossible to defeat, sweeping darkness across the land like the Nothing in the 1980s classic film, *The Neverending Story*. (Just Googled that movie to check the release date and wow, the wolf-like villain still gives me shivers!) But both can be controlled and even stopped. . .leveraging a healthy dose of organizational self-awareness and thoughtful, targeted work on working culture and, particularly, career paths. By giving some profound thought to how people should move through organizations, and what good *really* looks like in a given job, we can make work less greedy and stop ourselves from turning into pigs.

Seems like a worthy goal, no?

When Greed Is Definitely Not Good: The Rise and Continued Rise of Greedy Work

My husband and I went on our long-ago third date at a remarkable, now-shuttered New York City institution: Sammy's Roumanian Steakhouse. Sammy's was notable for a few things: live music accompanied by Borscht Belt–style comedy, vodka frozen in blocks of ice, freshly made chopped liver, and crazy-sized steaks that stretched beyond the boundaries of the plates they were on, flopping onto the table and defying a reasonable person to eat the whole thing (Figure 8.1).

What those steaks were to normal steak is what greedy work is to normal work. Greedy work refuses to fit on the plate of the workday, extending relentlessly onto the table of life and causing indigestion if you try to make your way through it all. Greedy work is, in its simplest form, working longer hours, watching your workday edge back into breakfast and creep forward through dinner and the evening. It's finding yourself responding to messages on the weekends and starting to treat Sunday night as routine prep for Monday morning. It's "working vacations" and staring into the blue glow of

Figure 8.1   Picture of Sammy's Steak

Source: TripAdvisor LLC.

emails when the dog's snoring wakes you up at 3 a.m. Sometimes greedy work assertively claims your personal time, and sometimes it just eats away at it. It can be both aggressive and insidious.

The idea of greedy work actually slightly predates Sammy's oversized steaks: while the Roumanian meat palace opened in 1975, per the *New York Times*, sociologist Lewis Coser came up with the term "greedy institutions" in 1974 "to describe institutions that 'seek exclusive and undivided loyalty.'"[1] Coser wasn't actually talking about bankers and consultants; his work examined groups like court eunuchs and members of a Leninist collective. (As a consultant myself, these comparisons are striking.) The common thread in these roles, per Marianne Egger de Campo, is "the lack of external coercion and the unlimited claim made on all of the individual's cathectical (i.e., mental and emotional) energy."[2] In other words, people were giving up their whole lives to serve someone else. . .and no one was strictly *making* them do it (Figure 8.2).

Interestingly, this strange and some would say, cult-like set of behaviors hasn't affected the entire economy. *Average* hours per week worked across all professions hasn't moved meaningfully since 1970.[3]

However, what used to be a penalty for overwork has become a premium. Four decades ago, if you worked more than 50 hours a week, you made 15% less per hour; today, if you work 50 hours or more per week, you make 8% *more*.[4] What this pay premium for overwork reflects is that mainstream "good jobs" doing white-collar knowledge work, including leadership roles, have gone from manageable filets to Sammy's-style distended sirloins. The Harvard economist Claudia Goldin, has been instrumental in investigating the "greedy work" phenomenon in this period, including noting recently that some of the gains in flexibility made during the COVID-19 period have the potential to mitigate the impacts of greedy work. Even Goldin, who's made a career in studying greedy work, admits the underlying causes of this phenomenon can be a bit murky.[5]

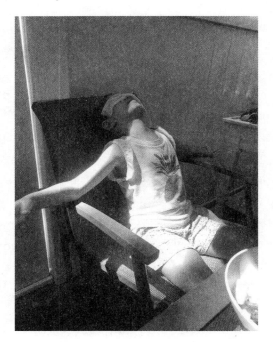

Figure 8.2   Don't let greedy work ruin your vacation!

It is worth spending a few minutes, then, trying to unpack the "why" of greedy work because the "why" matters if we intend to stop this phenomenon in its tracks. The *New York Times* offers an array of possible causes:

> Technology is one reason for the change, researchers say; workers are now more easily reachable and can do more work remotely. Also, business has become more global, so people are working across time zones. A big driver is the widening gap between the highest and lowest earners, and increasingly unstable employment. More jobs requiring advanced degrees are up-or-out—make partner or leave, for example. Even if they aren't, work has become more competitive, and long hours have become a status symbol.[5]

There's a lot in there. Let's break down some of the different pieces the article cites:

- *Technological change enabling more hours of work.* While always-on work tech is an easy scapegoat for longer hours of work, this reason is, sadly, a cop-out. Technology could just as easily have made work easier and quicker: What happened to the George Jetson world of sitting at work pressing a single button? (I'm endlessly fascinated with the fact that despite having an absurdly easy job, Jetson is just as stressed out as anyone and fights constantly with his boss. I may write my next book about this topic.) Even always-on technology can be turned on and off at will; it's dopey human behavior stretching out the workday.

- *Globalization requiring work at different hours.* Unlike technology, globalization *can* reasonably be blamed for some proportion of the greedy work phenomenon. The simple, immutable fact of time zone differences means you cannot dodge a stretched workday if people on different continents are going to connect synchronously. Certain cities sit at tricky time distances from each other; I've personally always struggled with the 11- or 12-hour difference between New York and Japan or China, which means in a best-case scenario both parties will be slightly outside classic working hours on one side or another, and in a worst-case scenario it's godawfully late or early for one person or the other. Because cities are not distributed evenly around the globe, there are "haves" and "have nots" in the time zone game. Workers in London often effortlessly bridge time zones, while their counterparts in Delhi at least benefit from handoffs back and forth at the beginning and end of their workday from U.S. colleagues. In contrast, the U.S. West Coast sits grumpy and bleary-eyed through early-morning meetings insensitively scheduled by their East Coast and European colleagues, and if you happen to be in New Zealand. . .oh, my. (I was in fact introduced to the notion of time zone inclusion by a long-ago boss from New Zealand, who'd suffered through too many meetings at insane hours and was determined that the next generation would behave differently.)

Working globally can often make inhuman greedy work demands on the people doing it. Forget stretched workdays: per the World Clock Meeting Planner,[6] if you're trying to schedule a meeting with Tokyo, Delhi, New York, and Auckland, there is literally no time available outside of traditional sleeping hours to do so. If it's a reasonable 8 a.m. in New York, it's midnight in Auckland. In Delhi, 12:30 p.m. translates to 3 a.m. in New York. A 7 p.m. meeting in Tokyo has New York up at 6 a.m. *and* Auckland up at 11 p.m. (and frankly, the person in Tokyo might want to eat dinner during that 7 p.m. slot too). And so on.

- *Unstable employment in "up or out" professions/work being more competitive/long hours as a badge of honor.* As Goldin explains in *Harvard Business Review,* in any organization where you are compelled to advance or risk losing your job, greedy work abounds: "Most firms and institutions with positions that are 'up or out' and that involve making partner, getting tenure, or achieving a major promotion will give rise to the type of greediness I've mentioned."[7] Where ambitious people compete for scarce resources, working more hours (and being more responsive to more extreme requests, from managers or clients/customers) seems to become a go-to strategy to distinguish oneself from the pack. But again, *why* would this be an optimal strategy? Research tells us that productivity begins to decline after 50 hours of work a week, and that after 55 hours, your work effectively has no impact at all![8] Particularly given what we know about diminished productivity beyond 55 hours, why would we reward employees doing what is likely to be lower quality or even zero-impact work a certain, meaningful fraction of the time?

This last one, in particular, is a real head-scratcher. So to better understand the greedy work puzzle, let's use the lens of *cui bono*—Latin for "who benefits?" Let's look through the dual lens we use throughout this book, from the perspectives of both employer and employee.

- *Who benefits from greedy work from the employer's perspective?* The perceived (and I'm saying *perceived* for a reason here) benefits to an employer from greedy work are actually pretty straightforward, when we put this phenomenon in context of the discussion in Chapter 1 of this book around intensified, performative, and misunderstood work. Employers with a strict eye on the bottom line, "managing by spreadsheet," will see overworked salaried employees as a positive, as long as attrition doesn't spike in some way. Think of it this way: If you pay Jane and Bob each $150,000 a year, and Bob works 70 hours a week while Jane works 50, doesn't Bob just seem like a better value play? If you're unaware of the productivity- and health-destroying consequences of intensified work, insensitive to how much performative work Bob is engaging in (sending emails at late hours just to show he's up and working, for instance), and the manager on the wrong end of misunderstood work (so you're not exactly clear what it is Bob does all day, anyway!), you're going to do the brute force calculation that Bob's just, well, a more dedicated and valuable employee. You'll see the world this way even if Bob's work has less impact than Jane's. . .because the actual *impact* of work is something you struggle to measure (per challenges in managing performance in Chapter 6). As a consequence, you promote Bob, who then views the next generation of Bobs and Janes through the same lens you did, continuing the cycle ad nauseum.

As you can see, from the employer side it's incredibly easy in well-remunerated knowledge work to let and, in fact, encourage people to work themselves to the breaking point. But what about from the employee side?

- *Who benefits from greedy work from the employee's perspective?* The answer to the *cui bono* question on the employee side is, I warn you, a bit more disturbing. (Though to be clear, you should become and remain disturbed about employers' continuing inability to measure the impact of work!)

To understand the employee's-eye piece, let's look at the other thing that was going on during the last 50 years or so, as greedy work took over so many professions. The percentage of women in the labor force has nearly doubled since 1970,[9] but the proportion of women in senior management roles has only risen to 31% overall—26% at CEO and managing director level.[10]

All of this being true, I'd argue that the rise of greedy work represents an unconscious but powerful move for groups that had been historically privileged to remain in that privileged position.

In general, the beneficiaries of greedy work tend to be male, often White, and generally already economically well-off, whereas the side that becomes disadvantaged tend to be female, non-White, and working to improve their economic position. The latter group is simply far more likely to have greater responsibilities outside of work and thus cannot engage in greedy work to the same degree.[11]

This argument may seem farfetched. But look at it this way: if, as women entered the workforce *en masse,* jobs could be somehow engineered to require something a meaningful proportion of women *couldn't* provide—an extraordinary number of hours per week—the folks who'd benefited historically by not having to compete with a broader, gender-inclusive talent pool could continue to comfortably rule the roost. And as the culture of overwork became more deeply ingrained, and pay began to correlate with hours worked in a way new to salaried employment, the advent of greater working hours also kept wealth in the same hands that had held it before.

I'm not arguing that any one individual decided to be a jerk and consciously bar the door to women's advancement. I am arguing, though, that now that we've seen the *impact* of greedy work on workplace diversity, we need to understand it both as a mistaken move by employers and a collective array of retrograde behaviors that keep us mired in a past of less diverse leadership and wealth distribution. Each of us needs to acknowledge our own role in perpetuating greedy work and in reinforcing the inequities it produces. For instance, a number of companies have begun to encourage men to take more leave when their children are born, to lessen the "childbearing penalty" borne (no pun intended) by childbearing women. If we all take appropriate time off when children are born, greedy work loses, and the world wins. There are a million such opportunities to establish healthy boundaries but a diverse array of workers—across genders, ethnicities, and wealth levels—need to all step up at the same time.

From Greedy Work to Piggy Bosses

Greedy work certainly contorts workforces and workplaces. But our second phenomenon, *Animal Farm* syndrome, is interesting because while it operates across organizations and is enabled through an array of processes, the end result is that it relentlessly reshapes *individuals*—turning them into less capable leaders at every step of their career journey.

To be clear, this isn't a chapter about the truly terrible bosses. There are a number of terrific accounts of that phenomenon, from Bob Sutton's *The No Asshole Rule* (the book I keep next to my computer at all times, waving it at people emphatically) to Paul Babiak and Robert D. Hare's *Snakes in Suits* (a definitive and utterly chilling account of how and why so many managers are actually clinical sociopaths). I cannot recommend these books highly enough; terrible management is a curse upon the business landscape.

Rather, this chapter is about the systemic forces that turn good, reasonable human-acting people into the slightly robotic managers they swore they'd never become.

So what is *Animal Farm* syndrome? With apologies for spoilers for George Orwell's nearly 80-year-old classic, think of the pigs at the very end of his iconic critique of communism. Having overthrown their farmer overloads at the beginning of the story, throughout the novel they've taken on more and more behaviors suspiciously reminiscent of the leaders they angrily replaced.

And at the end, they're physically indistinguishable from their former oppressors: "The creatures outside looked from pig to man, and from man to pig, and from pig to man again; but already it was impossible to say which was which."

This phenomenon, sadly, isn't limited to Josef Stalin taking on all of the worst behaviors of Czar Nicholas (and then some). We all do it—if you're a parent, you're incredibly lucky if some badly considered thing your parents used to say to you hasn't flown out of your mouth at some point. If you're a manager, you've likely found yourself engaged in some idiotic behavior highly reminiscent of a former boss—something you swore you'd never do when you got to a leadership role.

What's going on? Similar to the low-quality work produced by someone working 80 hours a week, it seems counterproductive that organizations would make choices that turn people over and over into bad bosses. No one benefits from this, right?

When we walk through a leader's lifecycle, though, we can see how a series of choices by organizations—both formal choices and pervasive informal cues—that seem optimal at different lifecycle points actually *shape leaders into the wrong mold* despite, importantly, the best intentions of those leaders themselves (Figure 8.3).

Figure 8.3   Don't turn into this little guy

Early in Career: Linear Is Best

Unless you were born a curmudgeon, you likely started out your career full of bright-eyed optimism and a wealth of curiosity. But early-in-career roles are not designed for polymaths or engineered to spur intellectual curiosity; rather, most jobs low on the career ladder encourage you to be really good at one or two things. Get to be the "go-to" person for a particular kind of work, or on a particular subject, and you'll rise fast. The same logic extends across hiring processes too—organizations quickly begin to look askance at folks a few years into their careers who've made too many jumps between organizations.

The business school model is in fact in some ways designed to address this issue, providing a free "reset" for folks well-heeled enough to pay an exorbitant amount of money to take a few years out of the workforce in their 20s or early 30s. (I'm pro–business school, but the model is not the most inclusive, to put it mildly.) That said, even with the credentialing a top-tier business school provides, early-in-career workers may struggle to shift their professional focus. In business school, I made a transition from advertising to financial services and still smart at the memory of a major bank's interviewer telling a friend of mine, "You know I just interviewed a girl from advertising? What a joke!"

That girl was me. *Ouch!*

Huge credit to Morgan Stanley, who did hire me for that summer internship, and Deutsche Bank, who hired me full-time post-MBA. Both institutions were apparently able to absorb someone from a slightly different career path without the world coming to an end! In both cases, allyship mattered tremendously, as fairly senior men from very traditional financial services backgrounds saw something in me that caused them to actively advocate for me in the hiring process. Their actions made sense in a business context: both organizations had such robust training programs, that combined with MBA learning there *really* wasn't a need for every hire to have worked in financial services prior. A hire out of advertising could bring creative commercial juice, which is much more difficult to train for than concepts like bond valuation.

Inspired allies and solid training programs aside, most organizations' early-in-career emphasis on highly linear skills-building and making few transitions between institutions begins to shape people's managerial capability in very distinct ways. If you're growing yourself in a linear fashion at a single place, you're not building the "test and learn" muscle we now consider so critical in a leader. When you're asked to put one foot in front of the other and please never, never step off the path, it's hard to develop any sort of tolerance for failure or desire to experiment.

Early in one's career, formal messaging about linear progression is reinforced with a healthy informal dose of a singular, very strong message: "Fit in!" The emphasis on fitting in starts early in talent acquisition processes; interviewing really junior folks with little or no career history to go on, interviewers often double down on the dreaded "culture fit" metric. I won't go too deep on the horrors of "culture fit," which has rightly been recognized in recent years as hugely problematic from a diversity, equity, and inclusion perspective. One excellent article on BBC.com showcases how silly hiring by culture fit can get, citing a bank that only hired lacrosse players![12]

I will note that hiring for culture fit has three troubling aspects:

- It generates homogeneous groups of new hires that resemble your current population (the lacrosse players).

- It pushes new hires who secretly don't quite fit the mold to "cover" and try to behave as much like the people around them as possible, sometimes prompted by pressure from those people. At various august institutions, I myself have been actively urged to wear different clothing and even carry a different type of suitcase. (I had the last laugh on the suitcase one: my supposedly weird clothing bag fit right into crowded overhead compartments even as my colleagues with rolling bags were agonizing over having to check their bags due to the bins being full. It's a great metaphor for cultural norms sometimes being dead wrong.)

- It ignores the role of "reverse onboarding," where you actually expect new hires to change the organization they're joining rather than those hires changing to fit the organization.

Considering the effects of these three phenomena together, early-in-career many people are thrown in with a homogeneous group, encouraged to behave more like that homogeneous group and encouraged to *not* bring their individuality into the overall cultural equation around them.

And we wonder why middle managers seem to act like such boneheads? Their early careers have been managed like one of those Play-Doh tools where you force a lumpy piece of dough through a mold and it all comes out in a highly regular shape.

But middle managers have their own forces bedeviling them and sending them even deeper into terrible leadership behaviors. Let's explore the world of middle management, shall we?

Mid-Career: P&L or Silo Is Best

When we talk about middle management, as Bronx legends Desus and Mero might say, this one hits different. I'm a middle manager. Many of my friends are middle managers. So, my absolutely, completely unbiased point of view is that most of the work of organizations is done by middle management.

I'm kidding, of course. But experts agree with me! Check out noted academic Zahira Jaser, writing in *Harvard Business Review*:

"[Middle managers] are the engine of the business, the cogs that make things work, the glue that keeps companies together. Especially as remote and hybrid work takes over—and the distance between employees increases—middle managers are more important than ever."[13] Gallup's *State of the Workplace* 2021 report found that middle managers were the primary driving forces of the productivity of an organization.[14]

Even as middle managers carry the weight of organizations on their backs, both formal and informal forces continue to deform their leadership styles away from the behaviors the companies they work for claim to want. On the formal side, middle managers are caught in a different vise than their younger selves. Instead of being encouraged to each be good at a single thing (which varies by group), they are generally pushed into one of two broad channels: general management operations or functional specialization. These categories are absolutely fine on their own, but they're missing two aspects that, were they present, would shape middle managers' behavior very differently.

Middle management jobs are in fact underweight on two of the skills that are most often cited as difference-makers in leaders' behaviors: strategy and true people leadership. You might say, don't middle managers have a lot of people reporting to them? Aren't they often tagged with a million and one strategic initiatives? Yes, and yes. But that said, middle managers' *metrics* are anchored in a very different world—one of basic operational performance, across a well-defined business or functional area. Middle managers are generally rewarded for hitting their numbers, not creating impressive strategic shifts or promoting and hiring game-changing groups of people.

Middle management jobs are also, definitionally, highly segmented. Remember the hoary cliché of a group of people unable to identify an elephant in the dark because they were each touching a different piece of it? Folks, that's middle management. We do a strange number on leaders, giving them little pieces of organizations to look at and then suddenly expecting them to make a jump to "enterprise leadership" at a certain executive level. Similar to the jump we expect from early career to middle management, where we want people to transition from linear skill-building to broader operational acumen, we want middle managers to magically take on a broader view when they cross a line of seniority, and then we get confused and start pouring in leadership development dollars when they can't easily make the leap.

Confounding the development of middle managers even further is a confusing set of informal cues: "the squeeze." The squeeze, in which middle managers have to balance fulfilling the expectations of the executives above them with the demands of the large talent populations below them, has been exacerbated badly over the COVID-19 period. The average worker's expectations have escalated, as studies like Mercer's 2022 Global Talent Trends show, while understandably, during a multi-year crisis, executives' need to achieve their goals has become more acute as well. In addition, remember Jaser's remark earlier, regarding the greater importance of middle management communications cascades in a remote or hybrid world. As middle management becomes an even more important communications channel, it pulls this group into more and more conversations, heightening the squeeze—and driving a more and more cautious and constricted leadership style. Become too progressive, or too conservative, and one group or the other is displeased. Being a middle manager can mean driving in a very tight lane.

Executive Level: The Noose Tightens

As the old adage goes, there are two kinds of hell: not getting what you want and getting it. By the time people have ascended to the executive level they sought their entire careers, norms for "the right" behavior have tightened even more considerably. As executive compensation has risen year after year, leaders at the highest level have more and more of an incentive, to, well, not upset the applecart. If your compensation is high, you might test and learn a bit and experiment with what works. If your compensation is vertiginously high, every mis-step has a higher perceived cost. . .and your personal conservatism might escalate even further.

This ever-narrower path is reinforced by mechanisms like executive search, which by the very nature of its business is forced to frame executive roles in quite narrow terms in order to execute searches for clients quickly. While the industry has put some emphasis on trying to source a more diverse array of candidates at the highest levels (reacting to pressure from business and society alike), the very economics of the search industry mitigate against this task. Completing searches quickly is the path to profitability, and expansive criteria for "what good looks like" in key roles cannot help but slow down, not speed up processes, even if a slower process might generate, well, better leaders.

There's a lot to unpack across career levels here, and some major rewiring to be done if we want to produce different leaders ultimately. But there are a few key ways organizations can get started.

What to Do: Organization Level

- **Strategy 71: Evaluate what you're seeking from your leaders at each stage versus structural cues at prior career stages, and seek to eliminate disconnects.** To produce truly different behaviors at each stage—from early career to executive leadership—organizations need to fix the structural cues in the prior stages. Put development aside for a moment, and look at things like how jobs are formed, how promotion decisions are made, and how pay is determined. What messages are you sending at every level—and do those messages shape people properly for the following level? Having a true career framework is helpful.

- **Strategy 72: Create more fluidity for junior talent, in both how you manage talent and how you hire for early-in-career roles.** Entry-level roles are, by their very nature, limited by the inexperience of the people who fill them. That said, with today's technology and real-time access to information, that limit is not set nearly as tightly as it used to be. Knowing everything isn't the foundation of a career anymore—knowing how to find answers is. With this principle in mind, many entry-level roles can be at least somewhat broader than their framing today. Moreover, as discussed in Chapters 4 and 7, organizations have the option of knocking down a host of barriers to talent entering, through measures like eliminating college degree requirements or conducting basic communications training for foreign-born workers. After all, early-in-career talent is still a relatively inexpensive proposition. Bringing in a wider array of capabilities and experiences, and then allowing those folks to do a more fluid array of tasks, can be an efficient reset on succession pipelines for the future.

- **Strategy 73: More love for middle managers!** Listen to them, team them up across siloes, make their jobs more straightforward, and reward them for the right things. That's all.

- **Strategy 74: Figure out *your* organization's drivers of greedy work, and seek to kill them off.** In *Anna Karenina,* Tolstoy famously wrote, "All happy families resemble one another, but each unhappy family is unhappy in its own way." Similarly, all organizations that have defeated or never engaged in greedy work resemble each other pretty closely in their balanced, nonanxious attitude toward work getting done, while each organization with greedy work issues has its own flavor of the problem. Determining what drives greedy work at your organization is a critical first step, allowing the organization to parse out legitimate causes (such as working globally) from more destructive ones (such as having a surfeit of leaders with nonworking spouses, who've never *had* to set boundaries between work and life). Once you've got the primary drivers of greedy work nailed, you can begin the process of turning them on their heads.

- **Strategy 75: Provide concrete incentives to combat greedy work.** As the data on greedy work and pay amply show, people engage in greedy work because we pay them to do so. It's not rocket science! As an organization, you have the choice to actually pay them to *not* work greedily. Examples of this include financial incentives for new fathers to take paternity leave and forced organization-wide time off.

While greedy work and *Animal Farm* syndrome are certainly organization-level problems, combatting them starts at team level. Here are a few areas where small behavioral changes can make a real impact.

What to Do: Team Level

- **Strategy 76: Model nongreedy work. Over and over.** I used to believe that modeling nongreedy work was a hallmark of smart, effective leaders. In my own career, I've been grateful for every leader (particularly the men!) who visibly stated things like, "I'm leaving early. I have [my kid's softball game, my seder, my dog's vet appointment, etc.]." I still believe this, but having recently done some work with talented veteran leaders at a major professional services organization, let me add another adjective to the mix—modeling nongreedy work is a hallmark of smart, effective, *happy* leaders. And folks, this is what sells it: there is no better argument for eschewing greedy work than leaders being visibly successful and *happier* working that way.

- **Strategy 77: Regularly "keep things out of the boat."** A classic brain-teaser sets up a situation in which a boatman has to get three things across a river: a wolf, a cabbage, and a goat. The boat only has room for two things in it, and certain items can't ride together (for instance, the wolf will eat the goat, or the goat will eat the cabbage). The key to solving the brain-teaser is figuring out the sequence of what items ride in the boat together at what times, such that each item eventually ends up on the other shore. Often with our working teams we're trying to navigate overloaded boats full of too many competing priorities that eat into each other—the boat's both sinking from overload, and the goat is blithely nibbling on the cabbage! It's a perfect set-up for greedy work, where hours expand as you're frantically paddling and swatting the goat back off the veggies. Figuring out what *doesn't* go in the boat (at least at a particular time—sequencing can be just as powerful a tool as overall deprioritization) can be the cornerstone of keeping work from expanding to fill all space.

- **Strategy 78: Think about your team members by career life-cycle stage, and consciously broaden their vantage points.** Particularly when we're under financial pressure, we often encourage people to do the narrowest version of their job. Get the basics right, we say, and everything else will follow. There's some deep truth there, and that's what drives some of the prioritization and sequencing we just talked about. That said, finding horizontal or diagonal stretch assignments for team members (in addition to the vertical stretch assignments that drive their journey in more linear ways) can counterbalance some of the naturally narrowing forces at each career stage.

- **Strategy 79: Don't let your own career journey shape your assumptions about your team members' (or potential hires).** Homophily—where we like people who are like ourselves—can be a powerful and corrosive force in the workplace. We hire in our own image, sometimes down to physical resemblance, and we encourage people already in our orbit to be more like us. We're also highly susceptible to self-serving bias, where we attribute our success to internal factors but any failures to external ones. Under this rubric, we make the well-meaning mistake of trying to press similar career choices onto our teams, believing falsely that our choices were the only factor in creating our success (and ignoring things like privilege and, *gasp*, luck, which often shape careers as much as any decisions made by an individual). To overcome these powerful sets of biases, you'll want to first understand what you believe your own career "story" to be—and to take a searching look at where things like luck and privilege played a role. I've done all kinds of things in my career that looked great in retrospect—my favorite being turning down a job offer from Lehman Brothers a few years before the 2008 financial meltdown—but where I can absolutely 100% assure you I acted with no insight or foresight. (The other place I was looking at just offered a more intellectually challenging role.) Knowing this about yourself is the first step toward giving others better, more unbiased career advice.

- **Strategy 80: Make sure you're not paying and promoting people for the wrong things.** This strategy extends across both *Animal Farm* syndrome and greedy work and is so basic that in some ways I was initially embarrassed to include it. However, it's a bad people practice that's so endemic across the business world that it bears repeating, one more time! If you're paying and promoting people for things like empty excess work or being narrow in an agile world, you're doing it wrong.

Reviewing the stylized career progression we've walked through here, it's really a wonder that any executive-level leaders turn out creative, broadminded, or agile. Structurally, the system rewards an ever-narrower path to success, encouraging linear thought and risk aversion throughout—even as greedy work pushes a more homogeneous group to the fore.

That said, work is changing now—and changing fast. We have an opportunity to grab hold of a far more positive future of work than ever before, which we'll discuss in Chapter 9.

9 A Good Day at Work, Every Day

Toward a Realistic, Human Future of Work

"It is better to have one person working with you than three people working for you."

—Dwight D. Eisenhower

Writing a book makes you contemplate a really deep question: *Why am I writing this book?* Even as I've spent countless hours on articulating the individual ideas in this book, I've continued to ponder this notion. What is the impact I'm seeking?

This chapter is all about that right landing place: the humanist change that *Work Here Now* advocates for. This change isn't an incremental move away from some of the less appealing practices of recent years, and it's not the articulation of a pie-in-the-sky vision of the future that we'll never get to. Rather, it's the beginning of a journey where organizations make more money by working with their employees better—where economics and empathy meet, and profit and employee happiness intersect and egg each other on. In this chapter, we'll look at some ways work is changing, generally for the better, and strategize about how organizations can get to a true future of work that is achievable today.

Asynchronous, Deconstructed, Transparent: Three Interesting Directions for Today's Organizations

Work is changing, that's for sure. You'd have to be hiding under a pretty big rock for the last few years not to pick up on that overall message. Everything from going to the office to how many days a week one should work seems up for grabs. Of the many changes, though, which are the most interesting—and meaningful? In my view, three trends really stand out: work is becoming more asynchronous, more deconstructed, and more transparent. I've spent considerable time with clients talking through these changes, which have mostly positive impacts but some areas of risk associated with them as well. Let's explore each area of change, how it's impacting organizations (for better and for worse), and what your organization should be thinking about to grapple with it properly.

Fewer Meetings: Asynchronous Work

Asynchronous work sounds complicated and novel, but it's actually something humans have been doing for eons: people working on things at different times. This could be nineteenth-century sewing piecework passing from one worker's hands to another, or two consultants on different continents making changes to a shared document during each of their working hours. One simple way to think about it: most of the time when you're working alone, you're working asynchronously. Two police offers arresting a suspect together are not working asynchronously; one police officer filling out the resulting paperwork, which will then be reviewed by her supervisor and the assistant district attorney, is working asynchronously.

If asynchronous work has been around forever, why do we believe it's "trending" currently? Technological enablement has been one key driver of this movement. Email made it possible for a document to ping pong from one person to another; the rise of Cloud computing made it possible to pass a document back and forth without gnarly version control issues. A need for greater flexibility has also driven a rise in asynchronous work. Even in arenas like manufacturing, where physical processes often seem completely dependent on both synchronous and in-person collaboration, organizations are working to pull apart long-held ways of working to enable a greater degree of asynchronous work—providing greater flexibility to both their workers and themselves. (If you're thinking that this example contains elements of the next trend—work deconstruction—you're not wrong! All three trends that we'll discuss here contain important links to each other.)

Asynchronous Work: The Benefits

- *Flexibility.* As noted previously, flexibility is perhaps the greatest upside of asynchronous work. When we don't have to work at the same time, or in a highly defined sequence, we have greater flexibility to work whenever and wherever we want. Asynchronous work practices that emphasize nonlinear processes, in particular, imbue tremendous flexibility to the employees performing them. If a team can all work on a key deliverable together without pressure to "hand off the baton" at certain points, it doesn't matter if team members are in Tahiti or working at 3 a.m.

- *De-intensification.* Definitionally, asynchronous work means not being in meetings. Thus, if meetings are the major force intensifying work in your organization, asynchronous work can dramatically lessen the burden. Per an article in *Harvard Business Review,* executives spend an average of a whopping 23 hours a week in meetings,[1] and 71% of those executives feel that meetings are unproductive and inefficient. Moreover, neurological research conducted by Microsoft shows that back-to-back meetings without breaks causes an unhealthy cumulative build-up of stress.[2] Disrupt the chain of meetings with some asynchronous work, and your brain has time to recover.

- *Globalization.* "Follow the sun" strategies—where a particular region starts working as another region clocks out of work for the day—become vastly more possible when work is made more asynchronous. Moreover, asynchronous work makes deeper contribution across regions possible. If decisions have to be made in synchronous meetings, it's easy for a particular region to take the strategic reins on a task and for other regions to be relegated to executing on decisions made many time zones away. Work truly asynchronously, and strategic decisions can flow organically into the course of the work.

- *Permanence.* The permanence of asynchronous work is a key benefit that truly had not occurred to me until I began researching the topic. Blogger and software engineer Andrew Knight writes, "Documentation *is* the unspoken superpower of remote teams. I strongly value written communication for its clarity, searchability, and permanence."[3] When you work asynchronously, the evidence of what you decided, and why you decided what you did, sticks around. In a blog, Levity CTO Thilo Huellman quotes Yac chief marketing officer (CMO) Hunter Moonshot: "Meetings and calls are perishable by default and since few are being recorded, let alone transcribed, all information is lost—instantly. Asynchronous communication allows anyone to comprehend the full reasoning behind a given state or decision now and any time in the future. Historical context is key."[4] The notion of a lasting record amid a cacophony of corporate noise is, without a doubt, appealing and useful.

- *Credit where credit is due.* Related to the notion of permanence is the idea that asynchronous work makes work concrete. Think back to the notion of performative work from Chapter 1—a good deal of performance occurs during synchronous work, where someone is there to watch! Kill off some meetings and make folks actually write down their thoughts, and you'll have a far better record of who actually did what.

Asynchronous Work: The Downside

- *Loneliness.* According to research conducted, critically, *before* the COVID-19 pandemic, the baseline state of work can be quite lonely. Research in *MIT Sloan Review* found that 76% of people struggled to connect with teammates, and 58% of those surveyed believed their working relationships were superficial at best.[5] Layer on a greater degree of asynchronous work, lowering the level of social interaction even further, and you may have a recipe for a large degree of alienation. We may see this impact played out in historical analyses of the COVID-19 period, but for now it's too soon to tell.

- *Miscommunication.* I have a funny, vivid memory of my boss from a long-ago internship on a trading floor shrieking at me, "Don't write an email! Get up and walk over there! Walk over there and ask your question!" She was onto something. For many people, their ability to communicate verbally exceeds their ability to communicate in writing—sometimes dramatically. (That said— there is some fascinating research that differences in written communication are a better predictor of effectiveness on the job, so certainly we should all strive to improve in this regard![6]) This is why email miscommunication is so pervasive, with 75% of respondents to one survey reporting that they had misinterpreted an email at some point or another.[7] Asynchronous work does make us more reliant on written discussion (perhaps not email, but in some form), so the potential for everything from minor "ships in the night" incidents to full-on angry blow-ups naturally escalates.

- *Silos.* Trying to work across silos is one of the signature challenges of modern organizations. I once asked an audience of 100-some leaders at a major financial services organization about examples of cross-functional collaboration, and someone actually stood up and said, "Cross-functional collaboration is a nights-and-weekends activity." As with loneliness, the baseline is already pretty bleak, and working more asynchronously can exacerbate issues. Take away synchronous connection points like meetings, and silo-breaking can go from extremely difficult to downright impossible.

- *Development.* It's a fundamental truth of human behavior: we learn from watching others. When work becomes more asynchronous, our opportunities to watch live how others do it diminish in some ways. Savvy observers will still extract a good deal of information from asynchronous work methods, looking at things like how software code changes to understand how more seasoned personnel are approaching challenges, but particularly early in career, many employees don't possess this skill.

Fewer Jobs: Deconstructed Work

There's something interesting in talking about work being increasingly deconstructed, when as we've looked at throughout this book, so much of work wasn't consciously constructed in the first place! So let's take a step back and look at what it means to deconstruct work; it's more than just ripping apart a bunch of aging edifices into their component bricks. My brilliant colleague, Ravin Jesuthasan, Mercer's global head of transformation, and his collaborator, noted academic John Boudreau, have enumerated four steps to thoughtful work deconstruction:

1. Start with the work (current and future tasks) and not the existing jobs.
2. Achieve the optimal combination of humans and automation.
3. Consider the full array of human work engagements (e.g., employment, gig, freelance, alliances, projects, other alternative arrangements, etc.).
4. Allow talent to "flow" to work versus being limited to fixed, traditional jobs.

When we think about work deconstruction in these terms, it is indeed going on all around us—at an ever-faster pace! "Taxi driver" is someone's whole job, while "rideshare driver" is a deconstructed set of tasks. Chatbots perform many of the tasks previously assigned to frontline customer service. At many organizations, internal talent marketplaces and even project sign-up boards allow employees to experiment with new kinds of work—not at job level, but task by task. Work is increasingly a tasting menu or a buffet—not a traditional series of appetizers, entrees, and desserts.

Deconstructed Work: The Upside

- *Fulfillment.* If you've ever wished you could take your job apart and keep just the good parts, deconstructed work is for you. Deconstructed work offers a true promise of greater fulfillment at work. Separate the working wheat from the chaff, and you can craft a workday that is truly satisfying to the human beings doing the work.

- *Efficiency.* Work deconstruction also has palpable benefits for organizations. According to various research efforts, useless work comprises between 5% of work (per large scale EU research)[8] and, alarmingly, 60% of work (as claimed by the late anthropologist David Graeber in his seminal and brilliantly titled work, *Bullshit Jobs*). Take jobs apart into their component tasks, and one cannot help separating the productive wheat from the useless chaff. Proper work deconstruction leaves organizations with just the work they want to pay for—and allows them to jettison what we'll politely call "horse pocky" elements.

- *New talent pools.* Conventionally constructed jobs, as we explored in earlier chapters, can be quite limiting in who can do them. Deconstructing jobs means that different tasks can go to a wider array of people—deployed in a wider array of manners. For instance, if some tasks are onsite and some tasks are offsite, separating them out from a single job means people with physical limitations, or simply people present in other geographies, can perform the offsite tasks.

Deconstructed Work: The Downside

- *The "many managers" problem can affect development and wellness.* In a more deconstructed environment, any given worker may be performing tasks that are ultimately accountable to an array of managers—including algorithmic managers, like the algorithms that assign Uber drivers to potential customers based on location and rating. Without a single point of accountability in the ecosystem, workers' needs for development and wellness can be diffused. We observe this today in any multi-project, multi-initiative environment—it's relatively easy to lose the thread on whether a particular worker's portfolio of work is impacting their wellness or developing them to the next stage of their career. To this end, Jesuthasan and Boudreau recommend injecting talent stewards into the system, a change I've seen implemented selectively at professional service firms already (and proof that job deconstruction isn't all about moving work to automation—it definitely creates roles for humans as well!).

- *Can lead to dehumanization.* Jobs are messy, complicated, inefficient, bias-laden entities, but they do have a strong psychological association with human beings. In our brains, one job generally equals one person, whereas a task doesn't necessarily carry a human association with it. Think of the name of a popular odd jobs service—TaskRabbit, not TaskHuman. For a discrete task, it's more pleasant to visualize a rabbit dashing in and out than a clunky old person. Tasks have a lower barrier to comfort with automation, which is not a bad thing; I might not trust a robot to care for my daughter across an array of needs, but I'd definitely let a robot fetch her snacks. (Please, please, please can someone invent this robot?!) The danger lies not in single tasks getting assigned to automation, but in the humans performing single tasks being *treated* like automated entities. For instance, once food delivery became largely disaggregated from broader restaurant work in New York City, workers had to press for legislation to *allow them to use the bathrooms in the restaurants whose food they were delivering.*[9] When a job became a task, the whole ecosystem seemed to forget that humans, with human needs, were doing it.

- *Tricky for wicked problems.* Wicked problems, as defined by Horst W.J. Rittel and Melvin M. Webber in 1973, are problems that resist solving through traditional processes. A *Harvard Business Review* article cites climate change or terrorism as examples of wicked problems—effectively, all the normal stuff you'd try to fix the issue doesn't work.[10] Accordingly, pretty much by definition, wicked problems defy work deconstruction because the very complex, task-interdependent, and iterative nature of a relevant problem-solving approach would mean you'd need to reset on tasks constantly and often unproductively. For wicked problems, a better approach is often to "hang around the hoop" as basketball players might say, making the problem the job, staying focused on it in all its complexity, and not trying to pull it apart into tasks that risk ignoring complicated interdependencies.

- *Disconnection from purpose.* In our work with organizations, Mercer consultants often parse out with employee audiences whether they see their role with the organization as a job, a career, or a calling. Similarly, the Japanese concept of *ikigai* states that greatest fulfillment is found at work once you can connect what you love, what you are good at, what the world needs, and what the world is willing to pay for.[11] Going from a job to a calling is a tall order and trying to achieve *ikigai* an even tougher one. Going from a task to any sense of purpose is even tougher. Think of the oft-cited example of the NASA janitor telling JFK that he was helping put a man on the moon.[12] Part of what helped that janitor achieve that state of mind was being immersed in the NASA environment, surrounded by other purpose-driven individuals. If he had been cleaning floors at NASA at an irregular, algorithmically generated schedule, among a host of other floor-cleaning duties, might the janitor have come to the same sense of purpose?

Fewer Information Gaps: Transparent Work

In days of yore, work was pretty transparent. With limited technology, humans could generally see every step of their work processes, be it making swords at artisanal scale or planting crops on a small farm. Scale and complexity created intransparent workplaces; a complicated supply chain distributed across several parts of the world and managed via an array of partners is in fact the antithesis of the small farm where you can see the growth of every plant. Today, organizations are increasingly using technology to reintroduce transparency to the workplace, aided by regulatory changes around topics like pay equity and pay transparency that mandate certain kinds of information being visible to working populations. Transparency at work might manifest in an array of ways; it could be anything from your being able to see the pay ranges for your job online to your having access via a dashboard to the same strategic decision-making information as your boss.

Transparent Work: The Upsides

- *Accountability.* Twitter Chief People Officer Dalana Brand states this idea in unambiguous terms: "Without transparency, there can be no accountability—and without accountability, there can be no equity." At Twitter, Brand has led a journey toward a transparent environment where everything from pay bands to the racial and ethnic composition of teams will soon be visible to every employee. Brand and the executive leaders she partners with believe that making the aggregate impacts of every personnel decision observable creates the appropriate pressure to do the right thing, each time. This idea can stretch far beyond employee data and decision-making—in the ESG space, it has long been a core belief that greater real-time disclosure of the impacts of company behavior creates more responsible behavior by organizations.

- *Empowerment.* If information is indeed power, greater information transparency is perhaps organizations' greatest tool to create empowerment all the way down to the front lines. Improved technology makes greater transparency possible, allowing workers to make better decisions for the organization and their customers. For instance, let's say a frontline worker is helping a customer choose between several models of phone. The customer is fairly agnostic among two options, but the salesperson has detailed supply chain information available on their tablet—and they can see that while one model ships immediately, the other is backordered due to a parts shortage with no end in sight. Greater transparency creates greater empowerment; with simple statements about phones being backordered versus not, the salesperson might urge the customer to go ahead and order the backordered model anyway, but with a better understanding of the supply chain problems, they steer the customer toward the in-stock model—creating a better outcome for customer and organization alike.

- *Access to new talent pools.* We often hire people for the information they bring in: knowledge of systems, knowledge of customers, knowledge of markets. This is an unavoidable dynamic to some degree because no organization can know everything(!). But by making existing knowledge explicit rather than implicit, greater transparency reduces the need to hire for information to an appreciable degree. In turn, hiring less frequently for information means you can hire more frequently among groups with less privilege—privilege, after all, often amounting to nothing more than access to information others don't have. This is an example of a seemingly neutral decision with palpable DEI impacts; you can make a straight-line connection, for example, between an improved customer relationship management system, better information on customers available to all, and being able to hire for salespeople outside of homogeneous traditional competitors. Choosing technology that drives transparency means more people can do a given job—and that's a very good thing.

Transparent Work: The Downsides

- *Loss of management control.* Empowerment, unfortunately, can play out in the short term as a zero-sum game, even as it creates a whole-organization lift at longer time horizons. When each level of workers has more access to information, this lessens the "information edge" of their direct managers. For managers with a more traditional leadership style, this can be uncomfortable because they can feel that direct reports armed with better information are challenging their decisions more often, or even directly contravening those decisions. This dynamic has been the genesis of hundreds, if not thousands of "digital leadership" programs, seeking to teach leaders how to lead with comfort in an environment where information is far more evenly distributed.

- *Bad reactions.* In a perfectly rational world, more information would always be better. We would receive each new piece of data with an open mind and take action along thoughtful lines. Unfortunately, per one of the core themes of this book, we're human. Human beings react to information in many different ways, some of them deeply irrational. For instance, throughout my career, across organizations I've observed ambiguously phrased announcements about new hires' roles serially riling up current leaders who wonder if their roles are being cannibalized. To be fair, sometimes this sort of reaction is in a way rational; information-sharing can reveal to a particular group that they should feel anxious or disempowered.

The changes being felt across more asynchronous, more deconstructed, and more transparent work are seismic. Organizations who tackle them head-on, rather than perpetually reeling from their impacts, have the opportunity to make these megatrends work to their success.

What to Do: Five Strategies for Organizations

- **Strategy 81: Deploy increased levels of asynchronous work to create greater flexibility—borrowing helpful practices from organizations where asynchronous work is more prevalent.** It's a rare organization that takes advantage of asynchronous work as much as it could. Instead, organizations rely on either oodles of meetings or archaically mapped, ponderous synchronous processes to get work done. To explore what work could be made asynchronous, one useful approach is to dig in with employees around where they feel they are spending too much time during their working day. If certain kinds of synchronous work "pop" in this analysis (say, status meetings), it can be quite straightforward to rethink the work to allow people to work more independently. To fuel the success of such a project, emulate practices from the software development world, where this mode of work has long been more common; these methods might be everything from teaching patience to educating leaders about talking to their teams less.[13]

- **Strategy 82: Teach better written communication skills to help fuel asynchronous work.** One no-brainer to enable asynchronous work in any environment is actually a basic that workplaces could benefit from across the board—better written communication skills. Think about it: Did anyone ever teach you, or any of your coworkers, how to write a great email? Might we all benefit from something like that? Absolutely! The better and more we can express ourselves in writing, the less time we need to spend working at the exact same time as someone else. Even for blue-collar jobs, better written communications help tremendously; think about how much more efficiently various processes could run if workers could succinctly communicate, in writing, the nature of a tech breakdown, for instance.

- **Strategy 83: Dig into deconstruction possibilities for "talent crisis" roles.** As the labor crisis shows no signs of abating, certain roles are facing catastrophic shortages. For instance, more than 18% of healthcare workers have left the industry during the pandemic,[14] and Mercer data projects a 3.2 million worker shortfall in healthcare over the next 5 years.[15] What can be done in critical roles like nursing? Well, in addition to measures like rethinking training to increase hirable populations, work deconstruction can be a powerful tool to combat labor shortages. Chopping jobs up into component tasks and shifting work around has the potential to dramatically alter the supply-and-demand equation for critical roles. Rethink what it means to be a "nurse"—and suddenly the work may be a lot easier to staff.

- **Strategy 84: In an environment of increasingly deconstructed work, explore novel roles with comprehensive talent accountability, especially with a wellness lens.** As noted previously in this chapter, Jesuthasan and Boudreau recommend talent steward roles to help talent flow to deconstructed work. In addition to helping facilitate a better match of person to task or basket of tasks, there is fertile ground to inject roles into organizations with accountability for the wellness of populations who perform deconstructed work. The idea is that people in these roles would look after individuals' holistic wellness, even as those individuals perform a diverse array of tasks for a diverse array of managers. Some Silicon Valley companies have begun to experiment in this direction, naming HR business partners responsible solely for contractor populations.

- **Strategy 85: Find opportunities for transparency to drive greater accountability and thus equity.** Today, organizations tend to find opportunities for transparency in one of two ways: they're mandated by regulation (such as in the case of pay transparency), or they decide to implement a technology that makes transparency easier (such as HRIS systems like Workday). We believe more "reverse engineering" should be going on: find a place where equity is lacking, and look at all of the ways transparency could drive accountability. Let's say a hypothetical organization's well-intentioned succession planning seems to keep generating identical White men for executive roles. What data, if it were visible, might truly prompt the people involved to make more diverse choices? Do they need to see performance rating distributions by gender and ethnicity/race? Do they need to see examples of anonymized comments on individuals that contain unconscious bias? If we believe that sunlight is the best disinfectant, where should the sunlight be focused?

As work changes, perhaps the greatest impacts are felt at team level—and that's where you can make some powerful changes.

What to Do: Five Strategies for Teams

- **Strategy 86: Use asynchronous work to make sure some meetings, especially standing meetings, die a gruesome death.** Every team has meetings it hates. Don't dismiss that hatred: listen to it. Identify your truly problematic meetings, and figure out a way to get the work done independently. You may have to test and learn; it might be easier, for instance, to use Teams than email, but you won't know that until you try.

- **Strategy 87: Create a team culture of "working out loud" so that asynchronous work doesn't inhibit development of more junior team members.** "Working Out Loud" is a technique popularized by author and consultant John Stepper to create better knowledge flow and community at work. My former colleague, Stan Garfield, explains it succinctly: "Working Out Loud is a growing movement that encourages employees to narrate their work and broadcast what they're doing so others can interact, respond, learn, and apply that knowledge to their own work."[16] If we can all get a bit better at "showing our work" and explaining how we think through problems, we don't have to do work synchronously but junior employees still reap the development gains of observing how work gets done. At team level, this shouldn't be too arduous—start by simply adding a sentence or two of explanation every time you do a piece of work and hand it off to someone. Inevitably, they'll ask questions and create a dialogue, building team-wide muscle in communicating around *how* work gets done.

- **Strategy 88: Make work deconstruction an everyday tool.** Work deconstruction can sound daunting. "Deconstruction," after all, is a 14-letter word, often used to describe pricey menu items at chichi restaurants. (I'll never forget my husband's amusement at a "deconstructed" borscht, which consisted of a single, tiny beet on one side of the plate and a tiny dab of cream on the opposite side of the plate—hardly the hearty, nourishing soup of his childhood!) In practice, though, work deconstruction can be accomplished very simply and regularly at team level—no culinary artistry required. As Jesuthasan and Boudreau explain, examining tasks for characteristics like whether they are repetitive, whether they require collaboration, and so on, allows us to better assign those tasks to the right person (or machine). Ask two simple questions: What needs to be done, and how does it usually get done? From those questions, a world of deconstruction possibilities opens up.

- **Strategy 89: Drive an open and ongoing conversation about the impacts of greater transparency.** This is another opportunity to ask a simple question: "How did that information make you feel?" Don't ever assume that information is received positively or neutrally, even when the information is something employees may have advocated to receive. Even seemingly banal information can sting under the right (or wrong) circumstances. Make sure employees feel they can talk to you about how increased transparency on an array of topics affects them—which means asking the opening question yourself, not simply "having an open door."

- **Strategy 90: Role-model asynchronous work, deconstructed work, and greater transparency in how you do your own job as a leader.** Want your folks to work differently? The absolute quickest route to that future is to model different work throughout your own working day. I can't tell you how many times clients have confided in me that their leaders advocate for new ways of working but work in defiantly archaic fashion themselves. It's as if you told your kids to eat their vegetables as you snacked on brownies right in front of them. What you do matters. Now, change doesn't have to be radical—some leaders may be comfortable working more asynchronously, in more of a deconstructed fashion (perhaps delegating key tasks for the first time!) or more transparently. Pick the strategy or strategies that works for you—and watch your team emulate them.

What's Actually at the End of the Rainbow: Toward an Achievable but Exciting Future of Work

When I talk to clients about the "future of work," there's a constant tension. In the wake of the most intense parts of the pandemic, there is a true and distinct hunger to do things differently: in our 2022 Global Talent Trends Research, 41% of C-suite executives agreed with the statement, "The fundamental shift in our business required a complete reset around work, the workforce and the workplace." Everything from labor shortages to a rocky digital transformation journey has made it clear to organizations that what got us all here won't get us any further. Every organization is, in some way, keen to change how they leverage their most vital resource: their people. My impressive colleague, Kate Bravery, has written extensively about "the rise of the relatable organization," organizations that succeed because, per our research, they do the things employees tell us make them thrive: making people feel valued for their contributions, engineering work that's fulfilling, creating a workplace where people have fun, and engendering a sense of belonging, among other things. Every single one of my clients, without question, has vocally expressed the desire to be a more relatable organization—and they mean it.

At the same time, due to the same difficult journeys across everything from pandemics to racial justice to just implementing a darn tech system that works, at this point in history, we're all realists. Engage folks at any organization about the exciting array of possibilities, and eventually you hit a point in the conversation where someone says, "This is all great, but what can we actually do today?" Especially as the economic future remains uncertain—with recession quite possibly on the horizon—the pragmatic beats the futuristic, every time.

We could deride this nagging voice as coming from a place of fear and incrementalism, but I actually look at this line of thinking differently. The quest for practical, implementable solutions that can be brought to bear right here, right now, is the greatest and most exciting aspiration we can have. For years we've grabbed for the lowest hanging fruit—everything from changing the titles of jobs but not the content to rote spans-and-layers cost takeouts to endless tweaks to pay without rethinking the philosophy of what the work is we're paying people for. We're in a moment now where we want to reach higher, so let's go for it. Let's bring the aspirational and the achievable together, marry up economics and empathy, and swing for the fences with our bats squarely in our hands.

Here are a few thoughts on how to do so, with a movie or TV quote for each. We'll start with my favorite movie from childhood— the only videotape we owned for years—*The Wizard of Oz*. At the film's conclusion, Glinda the Good Witch tells Dorothy, "You had the power all along, my dear," as all Dorothy had to do to get home to Kansas was click her heels three times. That's every organization—we have had the power all along. We just get caught up in day-to-day exigent business realities and don't take the much-needed step back to ask critical questions. Are we treating our human workers fairly? Kindly? Are they doing the right work, in the right way? Could we actually make more money if we did all of these things correctly? I'm betting on yes, and so should you. Believing you had the power all along is crucial.

On a related note, I'd also like to cite Oscar the Grouch here: "You'd be a grouch, too, if you lived in a garbage can." We spend an incredible amount of time these days trying to figure out why workers are quitting, when the answer is relatively obvious: because modern organizations were not built intentionally; in many cases, they are messy, frustrating, inconsiderate, and exhausting places to work. Sort some of these pieces out, and many of what we think of as individual issues—everything from broken performance to attrition to deep-seated needs for leadership development—would start to resolve with astonishing speed. We can, and should, build a better mousetrap—we could fundamentally change the economics of so many industries if we could simply get work done differently.

The final quote is, of course, from *Office Space:* "Human beings were not meant to sit in little cubicles staring at computer screens all day, filling out useless forms, and listening to eight different bosses drone on about mission statements! We don't have a lot of time on this earth! We weren't meant to spend it this way!" It's a hilarious rant, and it's also just deep-down true. As long as we believe work is supposed to suck, it's going to suck. Our deeply held beliefs that work should somehow be soul-deadening and even dangerous to our health are number one with a bullet on the list of reasons why work can be soul-deadening and often dangerous to our health. The dirty little secret is that these beliefs actually hold back things like growth, profitability, and productivity too.

Let's explore a world where work sucks just a little bit less.

Appendix: Strategies by Category of Action

This appendix lists all the strategies in the book by category of action.

Do

Strategy 9: Create metrics to measure and monitor work intensity.

Strategy 13: Map how your customer experience and your employee experience interact.

Strategy 20: Create a team mechanism for calling out appearances of the Anxiety Monster and the Boss Baby Customer.

Strategy 21: Create a "single account of the truth" on the workforce of your organization—however you employ them—and systems and processes to maintain it in real-time.

Strategy 24: Reinvent HR—on your organization's terms.

Strategy 29: Test and learn on disruptive approaches to getting work done, utilizing team contracts if helpful.

Strategy 36: Model humanism—including self-care.

Strategy 38: Plan like a pessimist.

Strategy 40: Have a few mental models for what "overwhelmed" looks like—and a playbook of strategies to address issues before individuals are in full burnout.

Strategy 49: Volunteer your team aggressively as beta testers.

Strategy 50: Make friends with your CIO.

Strategy 52: Cultivate thoughtful ways of managing performance by team or unit, avoiding the "hand-to-hand combat" of measuring individual by individual.

Strategy 55: Figure out which employee groups are "burnt out," and which are "fed up," and design differentiated strategies to address each set of issues.

Strategy 58: Identify your "talent competitors," especially those who are not your business competitors.

Strategy 59: Rigorously train on bias before each performance management cycle.

Strategy 61: In your DEI efforts, consider a broader array of populations, including foreign-born workers, previously incarcerated populations, etc.

Strategy 63: Understand the role of foreign-born workers at your organization, including the household workers who support your employees, and actively create support programs for this group (including naturalized/green card workers and workers on visas).

Strategy 66: Drive an ongoing, two-way onboarding journey— especially for diverse or nontraditional hires.

Strategy 67: Incorporate trauma-informed ways of operating.

Strategy 68: Cultivate an "immigration aware" mindset—including the foreign-born populations who work in the households of your team.

Strategy 72: Create more fluidity for junior talent, in both how you manage talent and how you hire for early-in-career roles.

Strategy 73: More love for middle managers!

Strategy 75: Provide concrete incentives to combat greedy work.

Strategy 76: Model nongreedy work. Over and over.

Strategy 78: Think about your team members by career life-cycle stage, and consciously broaden their vantage points.

Strategy 81: Deploy increased levels of asynchronous work to create greater flexibility—borrowing helpful practices from organizations where asynchronous work is more prevalent.

Strategy 82: Teach better written communication skills to help fuel asynchronous work.

Strategy 84: In an environment of increasingly deconstructed work, explore novel roles with comprehensive talent accountability, especially with a wellness lens.

Strategy 87: Create a team culture of "working out loud" so that asynchronous work doesn't inhibit development of more junior team members.

Strategy 88: Make work deconstruction an everyday tool.

Strategy 90: Role-model asynchronous work, deconstructed work, and greater transparency in how you do your own job as a leader.

Discuss

Strategy 3: Question long-held assumptions and unintentional choices about work to revolutionize your DEI strategy.

Strategy 6: At a regular cadence, talk to your team about their everyday experience of work—what are they doing, and how are they feeling, day to day and minute to minute?

Strategy 8: Be humble and curious about the parts of your team's work you don't understand.

Strategy 14: Tread carefully in how you talk about seamlessness and frictionlesness—internally and externally.

Strategy 15: Actively promote replacements for the anxiety monster and the boss baby customer.

Strategy 17: Talk to your team about pace—why are you moving at the speed you're moving?

Strategy 19: Talk to your team about their experience of your customer—whether they are customer facing or not!

Strategy 22: Maintain and periodically energize an organization-wide conversation about how work gets done.

Strategy 34: Make humanism an acceptable part of corporate discourse.

Strategy 44: Have an honest conversation about cybersecurity—and what it's going to *feel* like.

Strategy 47: Take tech gripes seriously—and *ask* about your team's experience of tech.

Strategy 48: Set realistic expectations around software and hardware.

Strategy 57: Regularly unpack the work/reward balance for your team, and teach them how to do the same for their teams—in real-time, not just at year-end.

Strategy 69: Continuously audit your leadership messaging about location in response to changing external and, particularly, labor market conditions.

Strategy 89: Drive an open and ongoing conversation about the impacts of greater transparency.

Examine

Strategy 1: Regularly reexamine work for signs of being dangerous (directly or indirectly), dull and annoying, or frustrating and confusing.

Strategy 4: Seek to understand work, even if it's painful.

Strategy 11: Unpack your foundational talent management assumptions—what decisions have you made on the basis of believing folks are lazy or slow?

Strategy 12: Regularly examine the jobs that impact your organization the most—have they changed in a way that affects how people's performance of those jobs looks (i.e., do they look lazy or slow because work is changing fast?)?

Strategy 16: Examine your feelings about your team—are you seeing them through an anxiety-monster lens?

Strategy 18: Examine whether you're inflicting anxiety-monster thoughts on yourself.

Strategy 23: Optimize how work gets done by different populations—tackling one chunk at a time.

Strategy 28: Turn your reasons not to hire into reasons *to* hire.

Strategy 31: Understand when you're making a decision that impacts your human workers, know who owns that decision, and identify who's truly impacted.

Strategy 41: Obsess over tech governance.

Strategy 42: Make sure you're choosing tech for the right reasons—and then make sure you're re-choosing it.

Strategy 45: Make sure tech is working at the speed of humans, and not vice versa.

Strategy 51: Rigorously and regularly audit your performance management results for bias—and be prepared to take dramatic action to address.

Strategy 53: Bring your contingent workforce up to "measurement parity" with your full-time workforce, including shared governance, capture in organizational systems, and centralized budgeting.

Strategy 54: Rigorously and regularly audit your pay philosophy and pay equity—are you paying for what you think you're paying for, and are you paying fairly, in real time?

Strategy 56: Confront your contractor addiction.

Strategy 60: Embed "everyday workforce analytics" into how you and the team work.

Strategy 62: Dramatically up the inclusion factor on your talent acquisition process.

Strategy 64: Take a searching, quantitative and qualitative look at your remote and hybrid work policies in the context of geographical talent markets, those markets' trends, and with a diversity, equity, and inclusion lens.

Strategy 65: Scenario plan your flexibility and location strategy versus possible changes in your talent markets as well as in the way we work.

Strategy 79: Don't let your own career journey shape your assumptions about your team members (or potential hires).

Strategy 80: Make sure you're not paying and promoting people for the wrong things.

Strategy 83: Dig into deconstruction possibilities for "talent crisis" roles.

Strategy 85: Find opportunities for transparency to drive greater accountability and thus equity.

Reduce

Strategy 2: Don't take intensified work for granted—and don't be afraid to de-intensify.

Strategy 5: Deliberately hold performative work in check.

Strategy 7: Quiet your "suck it up" voice.

Strategy 10: Take a searching look as to where you might be encouraging performative work.

Strategy 25: Just do less!

Strategy 26: Figure out your worst patterns—and have an honest conversation on how to break them within your team.

Strategy 27: Build your replicant—then destroy them.

Strategy 30: Not to sound repetitive, but just do less.

Strategy 32: Look at the key roles in your organization, and remove any unneeded qualifications or aspects of work that are limiting the talent pool of who can do that work.

Strategy 33: Smash your technology silo.

Strategy 35: Examine roles designed for obsolescence—do they have features you'd consider unacceptable in longer-term roles?

Strategy 37: Identify and obliterate "kludges" and temporary solutions that have accidentally become permanent.

Strategy 39: Figure out your hidden talent acquisition hurdles to maximize inclusion.

Strategy 43: Marie Kondo your tech stack—using an employee's-eye view.

Strategy 46: Agree on your comms tech.

Strategy 70: Look at how you can create dimensions of flexibility across whom you hire and how they work.

Strategy 71: Evaluate what you're seeking from your leaders at each stage versus structural cues at prior career stages, and seek to eliminate disconnects.

Strategy 74: Figure out your organization's drivers of greedy work, and seek to kill them off.

Strategy 77: Regularly "keep things out of the boat."

Strategy 86: Use asynchronous work to make sure some meetings, especially standing meetings, die a gruesome death.

NOTES

Chapter 1

1. Society for Human Resources Management. (n.d.). *Interactive chart: How historic has the great resignation been?* [online]. Available at: https://www.shrm.org/resourcesandtools/hr-topics/talent-acquisition/pages/interactive-quits-level-by-year.aspx

2. U.S. Bureau of Labor Statistics. (n.d.). *Productivity* [online]. Available at: https://www.bls.gov/lpc/prodybar.htm

3. U.S. Bureau of Labor Statistics. (n.d.). *National census of fatal occupational injuries in 2020* [online]. Available at: (2021) https://www.bls.gov/news.release/pdf/cfoi.pdf

4. Kochanek, K.D., Xu, J.Q., and Arias, E. (2020). *Mortality in the United States, 2019. NCHS Data Brief, no 395*. Hyattsville, MD: National Center for Health Statistics. Available at: http://www.cdc.gov/nchs/data/databriefs/db395-H.pdf

5. Bolotnikova, B. America's car crash epidemic. *Vox,* Sep. 19, 2021. Available at: https://www.vox.com/22675358/us-car-deaths-year-traffic-covid-pandemic

6. Society for Human Resources Management. (n.d.). *Workplace violence prevention and response* [online]. Available at: https://www.shrm.org/resourcesandtools/tools-and-samples/toolkits/pages/workplace-violence-prevention-and-response.aspx

7. United Nations. (2019). Stress, overtime, disease, contribute to 2.8 million workers' deaths per year, reports UN labour agency. *UN News,* April 18, 2019 [online]. Available at: https://news.un.org/en/story/2019/04/1036851

8. Kessler, S. (2021). Long working hours are leading to a rise in premature deaths, the WHO says. *New York Times,* May 18, 2021. Available at: https://www.nytimes.com/2021/05/18/business/overwork-premature-death.html

9. Schwantes, M. (2018). Study: The workplace is now the fifth leading cause of death in the U.S. (above diabetes). Here are the top 10 reasons why. *Inc.* November 21, 2018. Available at: https://www.inc.com/marcel-schwantes/study-workplace-is-now-fifth-leading-cause-of-death-in-us-above-diabetes-here-are-top-10-reasons-why.html

10. AFL-CIO. (n.d.). *Key events in labor history* [online]. Available at: https://aflcio.org/about/history/labor-history-events

11. Udemy. (2016). *2016 Udemy workplace boredom study.* Available at: https://research.udemy.com/wp-content/uploads/2016/10/2016-Udemy-Workplace-Boredom-Study.pdf

12. Marx, K., and Engels, F. (1848). *The Communist Manifesto.* New York: Appleton-Century-Crofts. Available at: https://www.bard.edu/library/arendt/pdfs/Marx-CommunistManifesto.pdf

13. HRD Connect. (2018). *97% of office workers feel frustrated at work* [online]. Available at: https://www.hrdconnect.com/2018/11/21/97-of-office-workers-feel-frustrated-at-work/

14. Lazar, J., Jones, A., Bessiere, K., Ceaparu, I., and Shneiderman, B. (2004). *User Frustration with Technology in the Workplace.* College Park, MD: Institute for Systems Research. Available at: http://citeseerx.ist.psu.edu/viewdoc/download;jsessionid=B6CCCA0F6E2459CF57B855EDE63722AB?doi=10.1.1.77.1411&rep=rep1&type=pdf

15. Bunner, J., Prem, R., and Korunka, C. (2018). How work intensification relates to organization-level safety performance: The mediating roles of safety climate, safety motivation, and safety knowledge. *Frontiers in Psychology*, 9, p. 2575. Available at: https://doi.org/10.3389/fpsyg.2018.02575

16. Green, F., Felstead, A., and Gallie, D. (2021). *Working Still Harder* [online]. Available at: https://doi.org/10.1177/0019793920977850

17. Paškvan, M., and Kubicek, B. (2017). The intensification of work. In C. Korunka & B. Kubicek (Eds.), Job demands in a changing world of

work: Impact on workers' health and performance and implications for research and practice (pp. 25–43). Springer International Publishing/ Springer Nature. https://doi.org/10.1007/978-3-319-54678-0_3

18. Federal Emergency Management Agency. (2019). Fire department overall run profile as reported to the National Fire Incident Reporting System (2017). *Topical Fire Report Series,* 20(1), p. 1. Available at: https://www.usfa.fema.gov/downloads/pdf/statistics/v20i1.pdf

19. Overhage J.M., and McCallie D., Jr. (2020). Physician time spent using the electronic health record during outpatient encounters: A descriptive study. *Annuals of Internal Medicine,* 172(3), pp. 169–174. doi: 10.7326/M18-3684. Available at: https://pubmed.ncbi.nlm.nih .gov/31931523/

20. Federal Emergency Management Agency. (2019). Fire department overall run profile as reported to the National Fire Incident Reporting System (2017). *Topical Fire Report Series,* 20(1), p. 1. Available at: https://www.usfa.fema.gov/downloads/pdf/statistics/v20i1.pdf

21. Bartleby. (2022, January 7). The rise of performative work. *The Economist.*

22. "The Rise of Performative Work," Bartleby, *The Economist,* 7 January 2022.

23. https://www.imercer.com/articleinsights/preparing-for-the-future-of- work-evaluating-the-effectiveness-of-your-employee-value-proposition

Chapter 2

1. Berger, W. (1999, Feb. 1). Lost in space. *Wired.* Available at: https:// www.wired.com/1999/02/chiat-3/

2. Lumen Learning. (n.d.). Available at: https://courses.lumenlearning .com/wmopen-introbusiness/chapter/reading-douglas-mcgregors- theory-x-and-theory-y-2/

3. Pew Research Center. (2016). *The state of American jobs* [online]. Available at: https://www.pewresearch.org/social-trends/2016/10/06/ 1-changes-in-the-american-workplace/

Chapter 3

1. Rudin, B. (1973). Industrial betterment and scientific management as social control, 1890–1920. *Berkeley Journal of Sociology*, 17, pp. 59–77 Available at: https://www.jstor.org/stable/41035183?read-now=1&refre qid=excelsior%3Ac252201a7bcdbe8d263e01e4ef06e3b4&seq=3#p age_scan_tab_contents

2. Consensus HR. (n.d.). *The history of human resource management* [online]. Available at: https://consensushr.com/the-history-of-human-resource-management-hrm/

3. Rudin, B. (1973). Industrial betterment and scientific management as social control, 1890–1920. *Berkeley Journal of Sociology*, 17, pp. 59–77 Available at: https://www.jstor.org/stable/41035183?read-now=1&refr eqid=excelsior%3Ac252201a7bcdbe8d263e01e4ef06e3b4&seq=3#p age_scan_tab_contents

4. Society for Human Resources Management. (n.d.). *SHRM certification* [online]. Available at: https://www.shrm.org/certification/ for-organizations/academic-alignment/faculty-resources/Pages/ THE-EVOLUTION-OF-HUMAN-RESOURCE-MANAGEMENT .aspx

5. Lindzon, J. (2015). Welcome to the new era of human resources, *Fast Company*. Available at: https://www.fastcompany.com/3045829/ welcome-to-the-new-era-of-human-resources

6. Lindzon, J. (2015). Welcome to the new era of human resources, Fast Company. Available at: https://www.fastcompany.com/3045829/ welcome-to-the-new-era-of-human-resources

Chapter 4

1. Johnson, C., Menendez, C.C., and Trout, D. (2019, Nov. 22). *Bathroom breaks.* Centers for Disease Control and Prevention NIOSH Science Blog. Available at: https://blogs.cdc.gov/niosh-science-blog/2019/11/22/bathroom-breaks/

2. Allison, K. (2011). *The effectiveness and enhancement of sleep deprivation as a tool in military interrogations to ensure optimum results and the short-term psychological and neurological impact on the prisoner.* PhD Dissertation, University of South Florida. U99275914.pdf

3. Bureau of Labor Statistics. (2020). *Occupational employment and wages, May 2020* [online]. Available at: https://www.bls.gov/oes/current/oes111011.htm

4. UNIVSTATS. (n.d.). *Graduation comparison between Ivy League members* [online]. Available at: https://www.univstats.com/comparison/ivy-league/graduation-rate/#:~:text=The%20average%20graduation%20rate%20of,complete%20their%20courses%20and%20degrees

5. Vom Saal, W. (n.d.). *Selected data on aging* [online]. Oneonta University. Available at: http://employees.oneonta.edu/vomsaaw/w/psy345/handouts/demograf.pdf

6. Schnitzer, K. (2019). *Data shows that going to an Ivy League school is no longer a requirement for Fortune 100 CEO.* TheLadders.com. Available at: https://www.theladders.com/career-advice/new-data-shows-that-going-to-an-ivy-league-school-is-no-longer-a-requirement-for-fortune-100-ceos#:~:text=Eighty%2Dnine%20percent%20of%20Fortune,%25)%20graduates%20from%20private%20institutes.

7. Schnitzer, K. (2019). *Data shows that going to an Ivy League school is no longer a requirement for Fortune 100 CEO.* TheLadders.com. Available at: https://www.theladders.com/career-advice/new-data-shows-that-going-to-an-ivy-league-school-is-no-longer-a-requirement-for-fortune-100-ceos#:~:text=Eighty%2Dnine%20percent%20of%20Fortune,%25)%20graduates%20from%20private%20institutes.

8. National Center for Education Statistics. (n.d.). *Fast facts: Degrees conferred by race and sex* [online]. Available at: https://nces.ed.gov/fastfacts/display.asp?id=72

9. Sammer, J. (2020). *Improving the lives of employee caregivers makes business sense* [online]. SHRM.org. Available at: https://www.shrm.org/resourcesandtools/hr-topics/benefits/pages/improving-lives-of-employee-caregivers-makes-business-sense.aspx

10. Steelcase. (n.d.). *The quiet ones* [online]. Available at: https://www
    .steelcase.com/research/articles/topics/privacy/quiet-ones/#:~:
    text=Introverts%20make%20up%2030%E2%80%9350%20
    percent%20of%20the%20workforce.

11. Aksenov, P. (2013). *Stanislav Petrov: The man who may have saved the
    world*. BBC.com Available at: https://www.bbc.com/news/world-
    europe-24280831

12. Zobell, S. (2018). Why digital transformations fail: Closing the $900
    billion hole in enterprise strategy. *Forbes*.

Chapter 5

1. Gabbat, A. (2021, Feb. 10). Texas lawyer, trapped by cat filter on
   Zoom call, informs judge he is not a cat. *The Guardian*. Available at:
   https://www.theguardian.com/us-news/2021/feb/09/
   texas-lawyer-zoom-cat-filter-kitten

2. Citrix. (2021). *The Citrix Smarter Workplace Report 2021: Volume 1:
   Demystifying hybrid work* [online]. Available at: https://www.citrix
   .com/content/dam/citrix/en_us/documents/analyst-report/volume-1-
   demystifying-hybrid-work.pdf

3. Fadilpašić, S. (2021, April 23). Workplace technology upgrades
   leaving employees frustrated. *IT ProPortal*. Available at: https://www
   .itproportal.com/news/workplace-technology-upgrades-leaving-
   employees-frustrated/

4. Lazar, J., Jones, A., Bessiere, K., Ceaparu, I., and Shneiderman, B.
   (2004). *User frustration with technology in the workplace*. College Park,
   MD: Institute for Systems Research. Available at: http://citeseerx.ist
   .psu.edu/viewdoc/download;jsessionid=B6CCCA0F6E2459CF57B85
   5EDE63722AB?doi=10.1.1.77.1411&rep=rep1&type=pdf

5. Gartner. (2021). *Gartner survey finds 60% of employees experience
   frustration with new software* (press release) [online]. Available at:
   https://www.gartner.com/en/newsroom/press-releases/2021-11-02-

gartner-survey-finds-60-percent-of-employees-experience-frustration-with-new-software

6. Cortellazzo, L., Bruni, E., and Zampieri, R. (2019). The role of leadership in a digitalized world: A review. *Frontiers of Psychology*. Available at: https://www.frontiersin.org/articles/10.3389/fpsyg.2019.01938/full

7. Weill, P., Woerner S.L., and Shah, A.M. (2021). Does your C-Suite have enough digital smarts? *MIT Sloan Management Review*. Available at:https://sloanreview.mit.edu/article/does-your-c-suite-have-enough-digital-smarts/

8. Gutelius, B., and Theodore, N. (2019). *The future of warehouse work: Technological change in the U.S. logistics industry.* Berkeley, CA: UC Berkeley Center for Labor Research and Education and Working Partnerships. Available at:https://laborcenter.berkeley.edu/pdf/2019/Future-of-Warehouse-Work.pdf

9. Forth, P., Reichert, T., de Laubier, R., and Chakraborty, S. (2020). *Flipping the odds of digital transformation success.* BCG. Available at: https://www.bcg.com/publications/2020/increasing-odds-of-success-in-digital-transformation

Chapter 6

1. Mercer. (2021). *Inside employees minds 2021 study findings* [online]. Available at: https://www.mercer.us/our-thinking/career/inside-employees-minds-2021-survey-findings-infographic.html

2. Pandey, E. (2020). Corporate America's revolving door for black employees [online]. Axios. Available at: https://www.axios.com/2020/11/17/corporate-america-black-employee-turnover-rate

3. Findlaw for Legal Professionals. (2017). Negotiating the hidden hazards of hiring contingent workers [online]. Available at: https://corporate.findlaw.com/human-resources/negotiating-the-hidden-hazards-of-hiring-contingent-workers.html

4. Fast Company. (2021). *Leaders: Here's how to make sure you're not excluding an important part of your workforce* [online]. Available at: https://www.fastcompany.com/90688293/leaders-heres-how-to-make-sure-youre-not-excluding-an-important-part-of-your-workforce

5. Foster, N. (2022). *How contract work drives disparities in tech.* The Aspen Institute

6. Johnston, K. (2013). *The messy link between slave owners and modern management.* Harvard Business School.

7. Nalbantian, H. (2021). *Value versus performance: how advanced analytics can distinguish between them and why it is important* [online]. Available at: https://www.mercer.us/content/dam/mercer/attachments/north-america/us/us-2021-paw-value-vs-performance.pdf

8. Levine, B. (2021). *Pay equity research series: Limiting repeat "outliers" year over year* [online]. Available at: https://blevinephd.medium.com/pay-equity-research-series-limiting-repeat-outliers-year-over-year-5be150b8c999

Chapter 7

1. Ferguson, S. (2022). *Understanding America's labor shortage* [online]. US Chamber of Commerce. Available at:https://www.uschamber.com/workforce/understanding-americas-labor-shortage

2. US Bureau of Labor Statistics. (2020). *Foreign-born workers made up 17.4 percent of labor force in 2019* [online]. Available at: https://www.bls.gov/opub/ted/2020/foreign-born-workers-made-up-17-point-4-percent-of-labor-force-in-2019.htm

3. Zaiour, G.P.R. (2022). *Opinion: U.S. labor shortages tied to low immigration in past two years.* Marketwatch.com. Available at: https://www.marketwatch.com/story/u-s-labor-shortages-tied-to-low-immigration-in-past-two-years-11642022353

4. Pew Research Center. (2017). *Immigrants don't make up a majority of workers in any U.S. industry* [online]. Available at: https://www .pewresearch.org/fact-tank/2017/03/16/immigrants-dont-make-up-a-majority-of-workers-in-any-u-s-industry/?utm_content=buffer 2d011&utm_medium=social&utm_source=twitter.com&utm_ campaign=buffer

5. Pew Research Center. (2017). *Immigrants don't make up a majority of workers in any U.S. industry* [online]. Available at: https://www .pewresearch.org/fact-tank/2017/03/16/immigrants-dont-make-up-a-majority-of-workers-in-any-u-s-industry/?utm_content=buffer 2d011&utm_medium=social&utm_source=twitter.com&utm_ campaign=buffer

6. Budiman, A. (2020). *Key findings about U.S. immigrants* [online]. Pew Research Center. Available at:https://www.pewresearch.org/fact-tank/2020/08/20/key-findings-about-u-s-immigrants/

7. Desmond-Harris, J. (2015). *What exactly is a microaggression?* [online]. Vox. Available at: https://www.vox.com/2015/2/16/8031073/what-are-microaggressions

8. Runyowa, S. (2015). Microaggressions matter. *The Atlantic*. Available at: https://www.theatlantic.com/politics/archive/2015/09/microaggressions-matter/406090/

9. Bier, D.J. (2021). *U.S. issued 1.2 million fewer visas to work-eligible foreigners since March 2020* [online]. The Cato Institute, Cato at Liberty. Available at: https://www.cato.org/blog/us-issued-12-million-fewer-visas-work-eligible-foreigners-march-2020

10. American Immigration Council. (2021). *Fact sheet: the H1-B visa program* [online]. Available at:https://www.americanimmigrationcouncil .org/research/h1b-visa-program-fact-sheet

11. Quba Ahmed, Muhammad Saleem Sumbal, Muhammad Naseer Akhtar, Hussain Tariq. (2021). Abusive supervision and the knowledge worker productivity: The mediating role of knowledge management processes. *Journal of Knowledge Management*. ISSN: 1367-3270

12. Batalova, J., and Fix, M. (2021). *Migration policy institute, leaving money on the table: The persistence of brain waste among college-educated immigrants* [online]. Available at: https://www.migrationpolicy.org/ sites/default/files/publications/mpi-brain-waste-analysis-june2021- final.pdf

13. Batalova, J., and Fix, M. (2021). *Migration policy institute, leaving money on the table: The persistence of brain waste among college-educated immigrants* [online]. Available at: https://www.migrationpolicy.org/ sites/default/files/publications/mpi-brain-waste-analysis-june2021- final.pdf

14. North American Moving Services. (2021). Where are Americans moving in 2021? [online]. Available at: Available at: https://www .northamerican.com/migration-map

15. Toukabri, A., Delbé, C., Miller, E., and Ozgenc, B. (2022). *Net domestic migration increased in many U.S. counties in 2021* [online]. US Census Bureau. Available at: https://www.census.gov/library/ stories/2022/03/net-domestic-migration-increased-in-united-states- counties-2021.html

16. Wilkerson, I. (2016). The Long-lasting legacy of the great migration. *Smithsonian Magazine.* Available at: https://www.smithsonianmag .com/history/long-lasting-legacy-great-migration-180960118/

17. Wilkerson, I. (2016). The long-lasting legacy of the great migration. *Smithsonian Magazine.* Available at: https://www.smithsonianmag .com/history/long-lasting-legacy-great-migration-180960118/

18. Muro, M., and You, Y. (2022). *Superstars, rising stars, and the rest: Pandemic trends and shifts in the geography of tech* [online]. Brookings. Available at: https://www.brookings.edu/research/superstars-rising- stars-and-the-rest-pandemic-trends-and-shifts-in-the-geography-of- tech/

19. Collins, M. (2019, Oct. 10). The abandonment of small cities in the rust belt. *Industry Week.* https://www.industryweek.com/talent/ article/22028380/the-abandonment-of-small-cities-in-the-rust-belt

20. https://www.chicagotribune.com/business/ct-biz-john-deere-fulton-market-20211213-mz5jf6y3azexpgunav7f4q4wyu-story.html

21. Carlson, K. (2022, Feb. 25). As farming goes high-tech, John Deere opens development facility in Austin. *Austin-American Statesman*. Available at: https://www.statesman.com/story/business/2022/02/25/john-deere-opens-austin-office-focused-agriculture-technology/6914135001/

22. Muro, M., and You, Y. (2022). *Superstars, rising stars, and the rest: Pandemic trends and shifts in the geography of tech* [online]. Brookings. Available at: https://www.brookings.edu/research/superstars-rising-stars-and-the-rest-pandemic-trends-and-shifts-in-the-geography-of-tech/

23. https://blog.google/inside-google/company-announcements/atlanta-office/

24. Couloute, L., and Kopf, D. (2018). *Out of prison & out of work: Unemployment among formerly incarcerated people* [online]. Prison Policy Initiative. Available at: https://www.prisonpolicy.org/reports/outofwork.html

25. Bucknor, C., and Barber, A. (2016). *The price we pay: Economic costs of barriers to employment for former prisoners and people convicted of felonies*. Washington, DC: Center for Economic and Policy Research. Available at: https://cepr.net/images/stories/reports/employment-prisoners-felonies-2016-06.pdf

26. Couloute, L., and Kopf, D. (2018). *Out of prison & out of work: Unemployment among formerly incarcerated people* [online]. Prison Policy Initiative. Available at: https://www.prisonpolicy.org/reports/outofwork.html

27. Root & Rebound. (2020). *California employers fair chance hiring toolkit* [online]. https://www.rootandrebound.org/wp-content/uploads/2020/02/California-Employers_-Fair-Chance-Hiring-Toolkit.pdf

28. Minor, D., Persico, N., and Weiss, D.M. (2018). Criminal background and job performance. *IZA Journal of Labor Policy*, 7(8). Available at: https://ssrn.com/abstract=2851951 or http://dx.doi.org/10.2139/ssrn.2851951

29. Son, H. (2022). JPMorgan says labor shortage requires unconventional hiring, including people with criminal records [online]. Available at: https://www.cnbc.com/2022/03/10/jpmorgan-says-labor-shortage-requires-unconventional-hiring.html

30. Root & Rebound. (2020). California employers fair chance hiring toolkit [online]. https://www.rootandrebound.org/wp-content/uploads/2020/02/California-Employers_-Fair-Chance-Hiring-Toolkit.pdf

31. Mercer. (2018). Thriving in an age of disruption: Putting people at the heart of change [online]. https://www.mercer.com/content/dam/mercer/attachments/private/gl-2018-mercer-thrive-pov-whitepaper.pdf

32. Berardino, M. (2012). Mike Tyson explains one of his most famous quotes. *South Florida Sun-Sentinel*. Available at: https://www.sun-sentinel.com/sports/fl-xpm-2012-11-09-sfl-mike-tyson-explains-one-of-his-most-famous-quotes-20121109-story.html

33. Manning, K. (2022). We need trauma informed workplaces. *Harvard Business Review*. Available at: https://hbr.org/2022/03/we-need-trauma-informed-workplaces

34. Centers for Disease Control and Prevention. (2020). *Infographic: 6 guiding principles to a trauma-informed approach* [online]. Available at: https://www.cdc.gov/cpr/infographics/6_principles_trauma_info.htm

35. D'Angelo, B. (2022, April 15). *Kentucky man who did not want employer to throw birthday party awarded $450K*. KIRO7. Available at: https://www.kiro7.com/news/trending/kentucky-man-who-did-not-want-employer-throw-birthday-party-awarded-450k/CSH56AQCRNGN5NFRP5A7VRZDEY/?outputType=amp

Chapter 8

1. Miller, C.C. (2019, April 26). Women did everything right. Then work got "greedy." *New York Times*.

2. Egger de Campo, M. (2013). Contemporary greedy institutions: An essay on Lewis Coser's concept in times of the "hive mind." *Czeck Sociological Review*, 49(6), pp. 969–987. Available at: https://www.researchgate.net/publication/266088268_Contemporary_Greedy_Institutions_An_Essay_on_Lewis_Coser's_Concept_in_Times_of_the_'Hive_Mind'

3. Rones, P.L., Ilg, R.E., and Garner, J.M. (1997, April). Trends in hours of work since the mid-70's. *Monthly Labor Review*. Available at: https://www.bls.gov/opub/mlr/1997/04/art1full.pdf

4. Gavett, G. (2021, September 28). The problem with greedy work. *Harvard Business Review*.

5. Miller, C.C. (2019, April 26). Women did everything right. Then work got "greedy." *New York Times*.

6. timeanddate. (n.d.). *The world clock meeting planner–results* [online]. Available at: https://www.timeanddate.com/worldclock/meetingtime.html?iso=20220406&p1=248&p2=771&p3=179&p4=22)

7. Gavett, G. (2021, September 28). The problem with greedy work. *Harvard Business Review*.

8. Sehgal, K., and Chopra, D. (2019). *Stanford professor: Working this many hours a week is basically pointless. Here's how to get more done—by doing less* [online]. Available at: https://www.cnbc.com/2019/03/20/stanford-study-longer-hours-doesnt-make-you-more-productive-heres-how-to-get-more-done-by-doing-less.html_

9. Catalyst. (2022). *Women in management* [online]. Available at: https://www.catalyst.org/research/women-in-management/#:~:text=In%202021%2C%2026%25%20of%20all,including%20six%20women%20of%20color.

10. Brenan, M. (2020). *Women still handle main household tasks in U.S.* [online]. Gallup. Available at: https://news.gallup.com/poll/283979/ women-handle-main-household-tasks.aspx

11. Magistad, M.K. (2016). *Got an authoritarian streak? Study says odds are, you're for Trump* [online]. The World. Available at: https:// theworld.org/stories/2016-02-25/got-authoritarian-streak-study-says-odds-are-youre-trump

12. Epstein, S. (2021). *What does being a 'cultural fit' actually mean?* [online]. BBC.com, Available at: https://www.bbc.com/worklife/ article/20211015-what-does-being-a-cultural-fit-actually-mean)

13. Jaser, Z. (2021, June 7). The real value of middle managers. *Harvard Business Review*. Available at: https://hbr.org/2021/06/the-real-value-of-middle-managers

14. Gallup. (2021). *State of the workplace 2021* [online]. Available at: https://www.gallup.com/workplace/349484/state-of-the-global-workplace.aspx)

Chapter 9

1. Perlow, L.A., Hadley, C.N., and Eun, E. (2017, July–August). Stop the meeting madness. *Harvard Business Review*. Available at: https:// hbr.org/2017/07/stop-the-meeting-madness

2. Microsoft. (2021). *Research proves your brain needs breaks* [online]. Available at: https://www.microsoft.com/en-us/worklab/work-trend-index/brain-research

3. Automation Panda. (2021). *Thoughts on remote work* [online]. Available at: https://automationpanda.com/2021/12/20/thoughts-on-remote-work/

4. Huellmann, T. (2022). *Why asynchronous work is the future* [online]. Levity. Available at: https://levity.ai/blog/asynchronous-work

5. Hadley, C.N., and Mortensen, M. (2020). Are your team members lonely? *MIT Sloan Review*. Available at: https://sloanreview.mit.edu/ article/are-your-team-members-lonely/

6. Byakutaga, B.N.K., Onen, D., Oonyu, J., and Kasesene, E.S. Written and non-written communication methods as correlates of employee performance: A study of academic staff of primary teachers' colleges in Central Uganda. *Journal of Education and Practice*, 7(10). Available at: https://files.eric.ed.gov/fulltext/EJ1099653.pdf

7. Lee, D. (2020). *When miscommunication leads to work issues* [online]. CPD Online College Knowledge Base. Available at: https://cpdonline .co.uk/knowledge-base/business/when-miscommunication-leads-to-work-issues

8. Brierley, C. (2021). *One in 20 workers are in 'useless' jobs—far fewer than previously thought*. Phys.org. Available at: https://phys.org/news/2021-06-workers-useless-jobs-previously-thought.html

9. Aponte, C.I. (2022). *The city, delivery workers cheer restroom access and tip transparency alongside AOC and Chuck Schumer* [online]. Available at: https://www.thecity.nyc/work/2022/1/23/22898143/delivery-workers-restroom-access-aoc-schumer

10. Camillus, J.C. (2008, May). Strategy as a wicked problem. *Harvard Business Review*. Available at: https://hbr.org/2008/05/strategy-as-a-wicked-problem

11. Eatough, E. (2021). *What is ikigai and how can it change my life?* [online]. Available at: https://www.betterup.com/blog/what-is-ikigai

12. Nemo, D. (2014). What a NASA janitor can teach us about living a bigger life. *The Business Journals*. Available at: https://www.bizjournals .com/bizjournals/how-to/growth-strategies/2014/12/what-a-nasa-janitor-can-teach-us.html

13. Overby, S. (2021). *Hybrid work: 6 more ways to enable asynchronous collaboration* [online]. Enterprisers Project. Available at: https://enterprisersproject.com/article/2021/7/hybrid-work-6-best-practices-asynchronous-collaboration

14. Russell, D. (2022). *WBUR Endless Thread, Nurses on Reddit are fighting for a better health care system* [online]. Available at: https://www.wbur.org/endlessthread/2022/05/27/nurses-reddit

15. Mercer. (2021). *U.S. healthcare labor market* [online]. Available at: https://www.mercer.us/content/dam/mercer/assets/content-images/ north-america/united-states/us-healthcare-news/us-2021-healthcare- labor-market-whitepaper.pdf

16. Garfield, S. (2018). *Working out loud revisited* [online]. Available at: https://stangarfield.medium.com/working-out-loud-revisited- 3c0c6c6b567f

ACKNOWLEDGMENTS

First, foremost, front, and center, I want to thank my husband Artem and my daughter Mira. Thank you for providing inspiration and support as I wrote this book across nights, weekends, and family trips. I love you guys very much. And thanks Mom, too, for everything.

Second, Mercer. I joined an amazing organization not long before starting to write this book, and I've been grateful for all of the help I've gotten as I simultaneously wrote and on-boarded to an exciting and challenging role. Susan Haberman and Ravin Jesuthasan have been incredible guides on this journey—I hope I can provide some serious ROI on your investment in me. Thanks as well to Ilya Bonic and Pat Tomlinson, who helped bring me to a terrific place to work, and continue to advocate for our Transformation practice, and thanks to the entire US&C Career Leadership team for influencing my thinking for the better every day. Our killer PR team (Lindsay Pracht, Cassie Lenski, Katherine Ratcliffe, and Micaela McPadden) has made sure to keep our best thinking in the headlines. Anna Vivas, Stephen Botsford, Carey Hoch, Jenny Hans, and Danielle Guzman helped get this book out into the world. Kevin Poff and Lisa Stella provided excellent chapter edits and also day-to-day moral support, and Dhara Singh was the brains behind Chapter 7. Tim Flank drove the insightful HR Scanner research I cite; Adam Pressman, Garry Spinks, Patrick Hyland, and the rest of our amazing Employee Listening team were the brains behind Inside Employees' Minds and other employee research referenced; Kate Bravery and Lauren Mason engineered so much of the Mercer research on how the world of work is changing that I was able to draw from. Shoutout to Workforce Strategy and Analytics, who inspire me every day. I'm grateful for our Transformation practitioners and incredible clients, who bring this work to life to make a real difference for organizations and employees alike. Finally, thanks to Martine Ferland, our CEO, for providing an exciting look at life with no glass ceiling.

Finally, the rest of the village. Zach Schisgal and the incredible Wiley team believed that a book was lurking in my brain, and brought it to life. Ginny Hamilton bugged me to write a book, and I'm so glad she did. Maria Amato and Michelle Stuntz were with me virtually through every day of the pandemic, not to mention the whole writing odyssey, and I couldn't ask for better friends. Mary Cianni is the fairy godmother of my career, not to mention a serious writing cheerleader; Mary Lawless has encouraged me to go be awesome throughout an almost 30-year friendship. Hannah Heyle and Jed Esty were amazing writing teachers, and I'm still a little in awe of both. My network at Chief connected me to the brilliant women you see quoted throughout this book. Birke Bakker, Joao Goncalves, Marisa Bolton, Tracy Bosch, John Pike, and Laura Kelfer were all incredible thought partners when my thinking was just starting to spark, each teaching me so much.

ABOUT THE AUTHOR

Melissa Swift leads Transformation Solutions for Mercer U.S. and Canada. In this role, Melissa is responsible for the firm's efforts in the areas of workforce transformation, HR transformation, HR digitization, diversity equity and inclusion, and workforce analytics. Melissa's work leverages data analytics, a healthy dose of pragmatism, and a humanist view of the workplace to create extraordinary outcomes for organizations. She has pioneered techniques to reshape organizations for digital and workforce transformation, leading breakthrough projects across industries ranging from manufacturing to professional services to biotech to consumer goods. Earlier in her career, Melissa helped build businesses in the ESG transformation space.

Melissa is a recognized thought leader on the subject of the future of work post-COVID-19: she has been quoted on the subject in the *New York Times,* the *Wall Street Journal, Newsweek,* the *Economist,* the *Washington Post, Axios,* and *Daily Mail* and has appeared on NPR and Al-Jazeera English. She received her B.A. degree in English and American language and literature from Harvard University, and her MBA in finance from Columbia Business School. Melissa lives in New York City with her husband, daughter, and dog.

INDEX